TSUNAMI

SUSAN BLACKHALL

TSUNAMI

SUSAN BLACKHALL

Published by TAJ Books 2005

27, Ferndown Gardens,
Cobham,
Surrey,
UK,
KT11 2BH

All notations of errors or omissions (author inquiries, permissions) concerning the content of this book should be addressed to TAJ Books 27, Ferndown Gardens, Cobham, Surrey, UK, KT11 2BH, info@tajbooks.com.

ISBN 1-84406-057-8
Printed in China.
1 2 3 4 5 08 07 06 05

CONTENTS

INTRODUCTION

I t was a disaster of nature but it was no act of God. The Tsunami that crushed and killed as it swept through South East Asia was more the work of the devil, the second biggest earthquake in recorded history, was dreadful.

The timing of this, the Boxing Day, with its holiday atmosphere of joy, hope and peace. The location literally fatally attractive. Thousands of holidaymakers were visiting their own special palm tree-trimmed paradise, complete with soft sanded beaches, sunshine and serenity.

The effect almost belied description. The deaths too many to calculate. Estimates have been between 250,000 and 300,000 but no-one will every really know. A host of countries and communities lost their lives and their livelihoods. Families were torn apart in every literal way, with parents having their babies wrenched from their arms as the monster wave stormed over them, and with news reaching far-flung places across the globe that a loved one was lost, never to be seen again.

No-one, it seemed, was untouched by the tide of tragedy that flung itself along the coastlines of 12 different countries. The tsunami was not just another disaster happening somewhere thousands of miles away to foreigners and strangers. It was impossible to remain detached. So many of us had a back-packing child who was there. We all knew of honeymooners, couples, families and friends who had gone to South East Asia to fulfil a dream of a long-planned trip, for retirement, or simply to experience Christmas in exotic surroundings. Above all, we all identified with the pain of loss or never knowing. It was as if the tsunami was no distance away from any of us.

If the immediate affect of the monster wave thrown up by the ocean was one of total despair, then the longer-term impact is destined to be felt for eternity.

Here is the story of the mayhem of a Mother Nature gone mad, the story of the Tsunami of 2004.

Right: *A view from a helicopter of the damage caused by a Tsunami in Phuket, about 862 km (536 miles) south of Bangkok, December 26, 2004.*

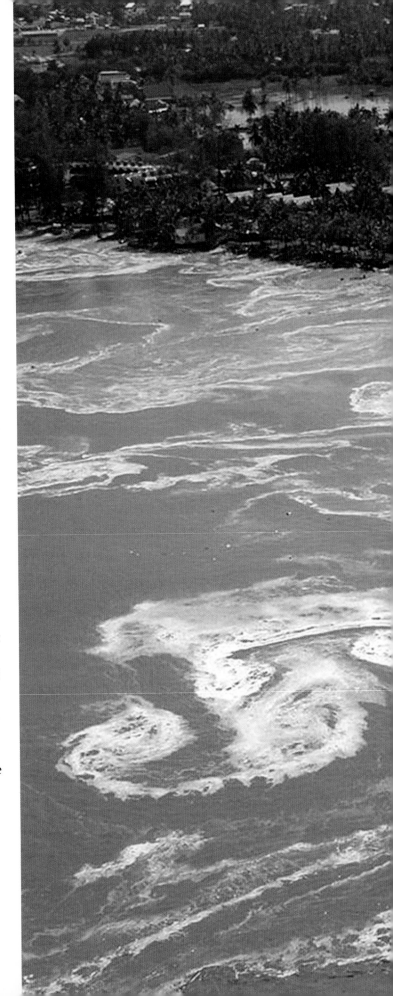

WHAT IS A TSUNAMI?

The word 'tsunami' has come into the English language only relatively recently. We all now know the awesome power of such phenomena. But what actually is a tsunami?

A typical dictionary description tells us that a tsunami (*noun, pronounced soo-nah-mee or tsoo-nah-mee*) is a fast-moving, highly destructive wave or series of waves that steadily increase in height as they approach the shore and are generally associated with movement of the earth's surface under the sea, by earthquake, volcanic eruption or landslide. Tsunamis occur most frequently in the Pacific Ocean but are a global phenomenon that can occur wherever there are large bodies of water.

The word tsunami comes from the Japanese *tsu*, meaning harbour, and *nami*, meaning wave. (In Japanese, the plural remains *tsunami*, whereas in the West it is perfectly grammatically correct to refer to 'tsunamis'.) The term *tsunami* was coined by Japanese fishermen who returned to port to find the area surrounding their harbour devastated, although they had not been aware of any wave in the open water.

The reason for this is that a tsunami in deep ocean is often undetectable. Offshore, it has a much lesser wave height (or amplitude) and a very long wave length, often hundreds of kilometers. Since they may form only a passing 'hump' in mid-ocean, they often pass unnoticed at sea. This, of course, makes them all the more unpredictable — and all the more horrific when they arise unexpectedly from the depths as they approach the shoreline.

Tsunamis were once generally known as 'tidal waves', although they have no real link with the tides. They were historically referred to as tidal waves because, as they approach land, they take on the characteristics of a violent onrushing tide rather than the cresting waves that are formed by wind action upon the ocean. However, since they are not actually related to tides, the term is considered misleading and

Below: *A frame from a video taken by an Israeli tourist shows an unidentified man clinging to trees while being hit by strong waves on the island of Kho Phi Phi, Thailand December 26, 2004.*

its usage is discouraged by oceanographers.

The causes of tsunamis can be several. They are a natural phenomenon generated when water in the sea — or even in an inland lake — is rapidly displaced on a massive scale, with effects that range from unnoticeable to devastation. Tsunamis can be generated by earthquakes, landslides, volcanic eruptions and large meteorite impacts — indeed any disturbance that rapidly displaces a large mass of water. However, the most common cause is an undersea earthquake. And here lies one of the reasons why tsunamis are so difficult to predict: for an earthquake which is itself too minor to create a tsunami might nevertheless trigger an undersea landslide that does so with devastating effect.

Catastrophes like the Boxing Day 2004 Tsunami are generated when the sea floor abruptly deforms and vertically displaces the overlying water. Such large vertical movements of the earth's crust usually occur at plate boundaries, and are particularly potent when dense oceanic plates slip under continental plates in a process known as 'subduction'.

Other causes are submarine landslides and collapses of undersea volcanic peaks, which are sometimes triggered by large earthquakes. As sediment and rocks slide downslope and are redistributed across the sea floor, the overlying water column is violently displaced. Similarly, a violent submarine volcanic eruption can uplift the water column and generate a tsunami.

Such natural events rapidly displace large volumes of water, as energy from falling debris or expansion is transferred to the water into which the debris falls. Waves are formed as the displaced water moves under the influence of gravity to regain its equilibrium and radiates across the ocean like ripples on a pond.

Tsunamis generated from mechanisms like landslips dissipate quickly and rarely affect coastlines distant from their source — unlike the oceanwide tsunamis caused by some earthquakes, as we have so recently seen.

Most of us are fortunate enough never to have witnessed a tsunami at first-hand. And, due to their sudden and unexpected arrival, even television footage rarely gives a realistic picture of the phenomenon . So what is a tsunami really like?

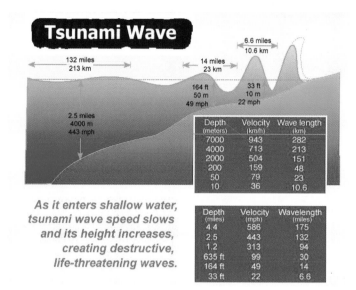

Depth (meters)	Velocity (km/h)	Wave length (km)
7000	943	282
4000	713	213
2000	504	151
200	159	48
50	79	23
10	36	10.6

As it enters shallow water, tsunami wave speed slows and its height increases, creating destructive, life-threatening waves.

Depth (miles)	Velocity (mph)	Wavelength (miles)
4.4	586	175
2.5	443	132
1.2	313	94
635 ft	99	30
164 ft	49	14
33 ft	22	6.6

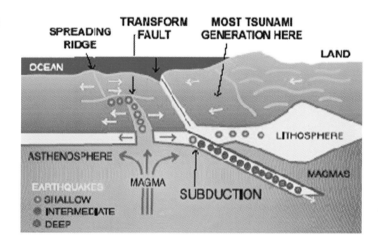

Well, what it is NOT like is the famous nineteenth-century woodcut by Hokusai, which gave the world the popular misconception that tsunamis behave like wind-driven waves or swells, lashed along by the wind behind them. In reality, a tsunami is better understood as a new and suddenly higher sea level, which manifests as a shelf or shelves of water. The leading edge of a tsunami superficially resembles a breaking wave but behaves differently: the rapid rise in sea level, combined with the weight and pressure of the ocean behind it, has far greater force.

Although often previously referred to as tidal waves, tsunamis do not look like the popular impression of a giant wave but more like an onrushing tide which forces its way over or through any obstacle. And tsunamis act very differently from typical surf swells: they are phenomena which move the entire depth of the ocean, often several kilometers deep, rather than just the surface, so they contain immense

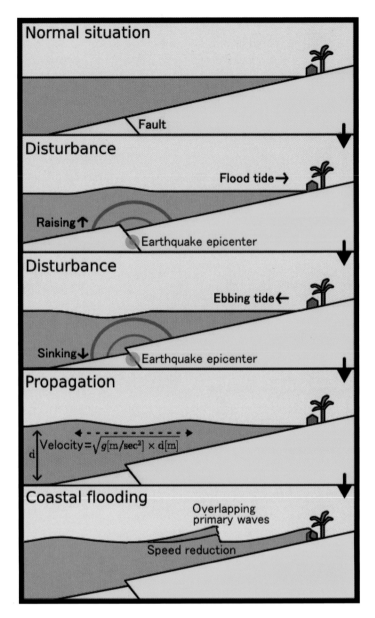

Normal situation

Fault

Disturbance

Flood tide →

Raising ↑

Earthquake epicenter

Disturbance

Ebbing tide ←

Sinking ↓   Earthquake epicenter

Propagation

$$Velocity = \sqrt{g[m/sec^2] \times d[m]}$$

d

Coastal flooding

Overlapping
primary waves

Speed reduction

energy, propagate at high speeds and can travel great transoceanic distances with little overall energy loss.

A tsunami can cause damage thousands of kilometers from its origin, so there may be several hours between its creation and its impact on a coast, often long after the arrival of the seismic wave generated by the originating event. And the overall loss of energy is small, although the total energy is spread over a larger and larger circumference as the wave travels.

Tsunami waves need not be symmetrical, so, depending on the nature of the source and the surrounding geography, they may be much stronger in one direction than another. As is obvious, they propagate outward from their source, so coasts in the

'shadow' of affected land masses are usually fairly safe. However, this is less than certain, as tsunami waves can diffract around land masses.

To further consider why tsunami waves are so different to 'ordinary' waves, one must consider a typical wind-generated swell seen at a beach. It might have been spawned by a faraway storm and rhythmically rolls in, one wave after another, with a wave length of, say, 150 meters at 10-second periods (the time for the next wave top to pass a point after the previous one). Tsunamis, however, have long wave lengths of up to several hundred kilometers and extremely long periods, from minutes to hours.

The actual height of a tsunami wave in open water is often less than one meter, and is often practically unnoticeable to people on ships. This is because the energy of a tsunami passes through the entire water column, from the surface to the sea bed, unlike ordinary waves which typically reach down to a depth of only 10 meters.

The speed at which a tsunami wave travels is a further mind-boggling statistic — traversing the ocean at anything from 500 to 1,000 kilometers an hour. That is maintained until it approaches land, when the sea shallows and the wave can no longer travel as fast. Instead, it begins to 'pile up'; the wave-front becomes steeper and taller, and there is less distance between crests. A person at the surface of deep water would probably not even notice a tsunami but by the time the wave approaches the coastline and compresses, it can increase to a height of 30 meters or more.

Just before the tsunami's arrival, the sea will be sucked back from the shoreline — in many cases, by half of the wave's period (being the distance between each successive wave top). If the shoreline shelves in a very shallow fashion, this recession can exceed many hundreds of meters. As happened with tragic results in the case of the Boxing Day tsunami, people unaware of the danger often remain on the shore out of sheer curiosity or to collect fish from the exposed seabed.

To understand the energy that the wave now

Right: *Two video grabs taken of large waves hitting a rock memorial off India's southern tip of Kanyakumari December 26, 2004.*

contains, one can take the analogy of the cracking of a whip. As a 'wave' travels down the whip from handle to tip, the same energy is compressed in less and less material, which makes it move more violently.

Technically, a wave becomes a 'shallow-water wave' when the ratio between the water depth and its wave length gets very small. Since tsunamis have an extremely large wave length, perhaps hundreds of kilometers, they behave in the same way as a shallow-water wave even in deep oceanic water.

For the mathematically-minded, shallow-water waves move at a speed that is equal to the square root of the product of the acceleration of gravity (9.8 m/s2) and the water depth. For example, in the Pacific Ocean, where the typical water depth is about 4,000 meters, a tsunami travels at about 200 meters per second (720 kilometers per hour or 450 miles per hour). As it advances, it suffers little energy loss, even

over long distances. But at a water depth of 40 meters, the speed reduces dramatically to 20 meters per second (about 72 kilometers per hour or 45 miles per hour). That is much slower than the speed in the open ocean — but still be difficult to outrun as it smashes into the shoreline.

From that point onwards, the sheer weight of water is enough to pulverise objects in its path, often reducing buildings to their foundations and scouring exposed ground to the bedrock. Most of the damage is caused by the huge mass of water behind the initial wave front, as the height of the sea keeps rising fast and floods powerfully into the coastal area. Large objects such as ships and boulders can be carried several miles inland before, mercifully, the tsunami subsides.

WHAT IS A TSUNAMI?

Left: *Video grab shows a tidal wave in Penang after Tsunami waves hit southern Asia on Sunday in this amateur video footage taken December 26, 2004.*

Below: *The aerial view of Marina beach after the Tsunami triggered by an earthquake in the Indian Ocean hit the area in the southern Indian city of Madras December 26, 2004.*

HISTORY OF TSUNAMIS

Tsunamis, usually set off by undersea earthquakes, have caused many major disasters in coastal communities over recorded time — and before. This is a list of notable tsunamis, including some floods that are merely suspected tsunamis...

35.5 MILLION YEARS AGO

The Chesapeake Bay impact crater indicates an inevitably resultant tsunami of unimaginable proportions. Created in the late Eocene Epoch by an extra-terrestial bolide (but undiscovered until 1983), it is the largest impact crater in the USA and one of the best preserved oceanic impact craters on the planet. The crater is 1.3 kilometers deep and 85 kilometers in diameter — almost as deep as the Grand Canyon and twice the size of Rhode Island. After impact, the tsunami engulfed the coastline and may even have topped the Blue Ridge Mountains.

6000 BC

In the North Atlantic, a major series of sudden underwater land movements over the course of tens of thousands of years are now known as the 'Storegga Slides'.

1650 BC

The eruption of the Greek island of Santorini some time between 1650 BC and 1600 BC is the probable basis of Plato's mystical Atlantis. It may also have been the basis of the Biblical Great Flood, which is recorded in Jewish, Christian, and Islamic texts. When the volcanic island erupted, a tsunami of between 100 and 150 meters was created. It sank the Minoan fleet, which was lying along the shore of Crete, 70 kilometers (45 miles) away, and devastated the north coast of Crete itself.

500 AD

A sudden surge of sea wiped out Poompuhar, once a prosperous trading city in the Nagai district of Sri Lanka. (It was to suffer further in the Krakatoa tsunami of 1883 and again in 2004.)

1524

A tsunami was recorded near Dabhol, in the Indian province of Maharashtra.

1607

A flood surged up England's Bristol Channel on January 20, sweeping away villages, destroying flocks and drowning thousands of people. The cause is disputed but might have been either a tsunami or a freak tide exacerbated by storms.

1700

On January 26, the Cascadia Earthquake, deep beneath the Pacific Ocean, with an estimated magnitude of 9, caused massive tsunamis across the Pacific Northwest and in Japan

1762

On April 2, a tsunami wreaked havoc along the Arakan Coast of Myanmar.

1775

The 'Great Lisbon Earthquake' generated a wave up to six meters that struck coastal Portugal, Spain and Morocco on November 1. Tens of thousands of Portuguese who survived the actual earthquake were killed by the tsunami that followed a half hour later. Many townspeople had fled to the waterfront, believing the area safe from fires and from falling debris from aftershocks. Before the great wall of water hit the harbour, waters retreated, revealing lost cargo and forgotten shipwrecks. The earthquake, tsunami, and subsequent fires killed more than a third of Lisbon's population of 275,000.

Above: *Devastation at Poompuhar.*

Lisbon Cathedral

Lisbon Opera House

Lisbon Patriarchal

Lisbon St. Nicholas Church

Lisbon St. Pauls Church

Lisbon St. Rocks Church

This copper engraving of the 1775 Lisbon Eartquake, made that year, shows the city in ruins and in flames and the followingtsunami devastating the port.

1819
On June 16, a tsunami is recorded as having hit the Rann of Kachchh (or Kutch), Gujarat, India.

1840
What Americans refer to as the 'Great Swell' on the Delaware River on November 14 is now believed by many to have been a tsunami.

1847
Great Nicobar Island, part of the Indian-owned Andaman and Nicobar chain in the Indian Ocean, off Sumatra, was hit by a tsunami on October 31.

1867
In the Caribbean, the Virgin Islands were hit by a tsunami on November 18.

Lithograph showing the waves at St.Thomas's, Virgin Islands.

The volcano Krakatoa east of Java.

1872
The Atlantic coastline of Maine suffered sudden wave damage on November 17.

1881
Car Nicobar Island, part of the Andaman and Nicobar chain, was hit by a tsunami on December 31.

1883
The eruption of the volcano Krakatoa (or Krakatau) generated a massive wave that swept over the shores of nearby Java and Sumatra, killing 36,000 people. The Indonesian island volcano exploded on August 27, with devastating fury, emptying its underground magma chamber and causing much overlying land and seabed to collapse into it. The earth movements impelled a series of giant tsunami waves reaching a height of more than 40 meters. They radiated across

Damage to Kamaishi Harbor, caused by the tsunami that followed the Sanriku earthquake of 1896.

the Indian Ocean and Pacific Ocean, reaching the American West Coast, South America and even the English Channel. On the facing coasts of Java and Sumatra, the sea flood went many miles inland.

1896

The Sanriku tsunami, one of the worst in history, struck Japan without warning on June 15. A wave estimated at 'seven stories tall' (more than 23 meters high) engulfed entire villages. Among the 26,000 dead were a crowd gathered to celebrate a religious festival.

1896

A tsunami washed away part of the embankment and main boulevard of Santa Barbara, California, on December 17.

1906

A devastating offshore quake on January 31 submerged part of Tumaco, Colombia, and washed away every house on the coast between Micay, Colombia, and Rioverde, Ecuador. The death toll was variously estimated at 500 to 1,500.

1913

Waves at Longport, New Jersey, on June 9 are officially listed as 'Possible Tsunami' in the records of the NOAA National Weather Service Forecast Office.

1918

A tsunami struck Puerto Rico on October 11.

1923

Triplicate waves on August 6 at Rockaway Park, Queens, New York, are listed by the NOAA as being indicative of a tsunami.

1924

Coney Island, New York, was hit by waves on August 8 that, according to the NOAA, were also indicative of a tsunami.

1926

Floods in Maine on January 9 have since been attributed to a tsunami.

1929

What is now known as the 'Newfoundland Tsunami' on November 18 was the result of an undersea landslide far offshore in the North Atlantic. It was caused by an earthquake of 7.2 magnitude which was recorded beneath the Laurentian Slope on the Grand Banks. The earthquake was felt throughout the Atlantic Provinces of Canada, as far west as Ottawa, Ontario and as far south as Claymont, Delaware. The resulting waves rose to more than seven meters in

Three pictures showing damage caused by the 1929 Tsunami in Newfoundland.

Aftermath of the 1929 Tusnami.

height. Twenty-eight people were killed when the tsunami struck the Burin Peninsula on the south coast of Newfoundland, all of two and a half hours later.

1931

Atlantic City, New Jersey, received tsunami-scale waves on August 19, according to the NOAA National Weather Service Forecast Office.

1938

A hurricane off the New Jersey Coast on September 21 caused waves listed by the NOAA as being indicative of a tsunami.

1945

The Mekran coast of Balochistan was hit by a tsunami on November 28.

1946

Tsunamis struck the Dominican Republic twice within a month — on August 4 and again on August 18.

1946

An Alaskan earthquake in the Aleutian Islands on April 1 generated a tsunami that destroyed North Cape Lighthouse, killing five. Hours later the wave arrived at Hilo, Hawaii, killing 159 people and doing millions of dollars in damage. The so-called 'Pacific Tsunami' had one good outcome: it resulted in the creation of a tsunami warning system, established in 1949 for Pacific Ocean area countries.

A tsunami generated in the Aleutian Islands striking the beachfront area at the Puumaile Tuberculosis Hospital on the Island of Hawaii, about 3,800 km from the generating area of the Alaskan Earthquake on April 1, 1946.

Tsunami damage caused by an earthquake in the Aleutian islands, Alaska on April 1, 1946.

A magnitude 8.0 (Mw) earthquake with the source to the south of Unimak Island generated a tsunami that destroyed the five-story lighthouse, located 9.8 m above sea level. April 1, 1946, Aleutian Islands, Alaska.

In Hilo, Hawaii, waves were 6.1 meters high, caused by the Aleutian Island Earthquake.

Wreckage of a political party clubhouse, Kamehameha Avenue, Hilo, Hawaii.

Tsunami breaking over Pier No. 1 in Hilo Harbor.

Lityu Bay 1954. Trimlines of the 1936 giant waves (G) and the 1853-1854 giant wave (K). Lateral moraines (M).

A giant wave generated on July 9th 1958 created by a rock slide from the cliff (R).

Aerial view of coastal area on Isla Chiloe, Chile, showing tsunami damage and wave extent.

Waiakea area of Hilo, Hawaii, devasted by the "Great Chilean Earthquake" 1960.

1958

On July 9, a huge landslip caused a record-breaking tsunami in Lituya Bay, Alaska — the shape of which influenced the freak effects. Local geological conditions gave rise to larger than normal shock waves (solitons), producing a megatsunami with a water wave rising from 50 to 150 meters. It travelled at over 100 miles an hour into fjord-shaped Lituya Bay — and reached a record 524 meters up local mountains.

1960

The 'Great Chilean Earthquake' of May 22 is the strongest ever recorded, at magnitude 9.5. It occurred off the coast of South Central Chile and generated one of the most destructive tsunamis of the 20th century. It spread across the entire Pacific Ocean, with waves measuring up to 25 meters high. It killed 1,000 in Chile and caused damage in Hawaii, where 61 died, and in the Philippines, Okinawa and Japan. When the tsunami hit Onagawa, Japan, almost 22 hours after the quake, the wave height was three meters above high tide. The number of people killed by the earthquake and subsequent tsunami is estimated to be up to 2,300.

1964

Seemingly freak waves that may have been due to undersea activity hit the Northeast seaboard of the USA on May 19.

1964

The March 28 'Good Friday Earthquake' in Alaska sent out a wave swamping much of the Alaskan coast and destroying three villages. The resultant tsunami was up to 6 meters tall, and caused drownings as far away as Crescent City, California. The full death toll of the 9.2-magnitude quake as it swept down the West Coast was 107 people in Alaska, four in Oregon and 11 in California.

Aerial view of Valdez, Alaska, showing the extent of inundation along the coastline. The town of Valdez was situated on the edge of an outwash delta about 150 km from the generating area in 1964.

View of the north end of Resurrection Bay at Seward, Alaska, about 75 km from the epicenter of the "Good Friday Earthquake".

Devastation following the 1976 tsunami in the Moro Gulf, Philippines.

1976

At around midnight on August 16, a tsunami killed more than 5,000 people in the Moro Gulf region of the Philippines, including Cotabato city.

1983

Spawned by an earthquake in the Central Sea of Japan on May 26, a tsunami killed 104 people in western Japan and claimed other victims in Korea.

Four pictures showing the tsunami Generated by the earthquake of May 26, 1983 in Japan.

1992

On September 1, 1992, an earthquake with a magnitude of 7.0 generated a tsunami with waves between 8 and 15 meters high that struck 26 towns along 250 km of Nicaragua's Pacific coast. More than 40,000 people were affected by the loss of their homes or means of income. The waves left 116 dead, 63 missing and another 489 injured.

On December 12, 1992, a 7.8 surface wave magnitude earthquake occurred in the Flores region of Indonesia. Flores Island is located about 1,800 km east of Jakarta. The death toll as a result of the combined earthquake and tsunami effects was more than 2,000. This slide set shows damage from the September tsunami along Nicaragua's Pacific coast and the December tsunami in the Flores region of Indonesia .

The beach area at El Popoyo, Nicuragua, after the tsunami. A large rock shown in the photo was carried from an offshore region 50 m inland and raised 1.85 m above sea level.

The tsunami damage at El Tranisto, (population 1,000), the area most devastated by the tsunami in Nicaragua.

An aerial view of Riangkroko after the tsunami. The area inundated by the tsunami appears as bare ground. The devastation indicates that the tsunami must have been very strong to have removed almost all the vegetation and structures in the area.

The effects of the tsunami at Wuhring, Flores Island. Although the tsunami heights at this location were lower than elsewhere (only about 3.5 m) the waves swept entirely over the 400 m by 200 m peninsula inundating the densely populated community of Wuhring and killing 100.

1993

On July 12, 1993, a magnitude 7.8 earthquake occurred off the west coast of Hokkaido and the small offshore island of Okushiri in the Sea of Japan. In two to five minutes the tsunami, one of the largest in Japan's history, engulfed the coastline of Okushiri Island and the central west coast of Hokkaido. Almost two hundred fatalities were associated with the event, with more than half attributed to the tsunami. The $600 million in property losses were attributed primarily to the tsunami. This tsunami caused spectacular localized damage, especially on the southwestern shores of Hokkaido and on Okushiri Island.

Previous page: *A view of the complete devastation of Pagaraman, on Babi Island, due to strong earth shaking and tsunami waves. About 700 people were reported killed and more than 100 were reported missing, following the earthquake of September 1, 1992*

Below: *A view of tsunami and related fire damage on southeast Okushiri Island in the community of Aonae.*

Above: *Debris scattered by the tsunami at Aonae, Okushiri Island after it struck in July 1993.*

Above: *A large 70-meters long barge was moved 75 m from the harbor by the flooding tsunami waves.*

The sand spit where the two Arop villages once stood.

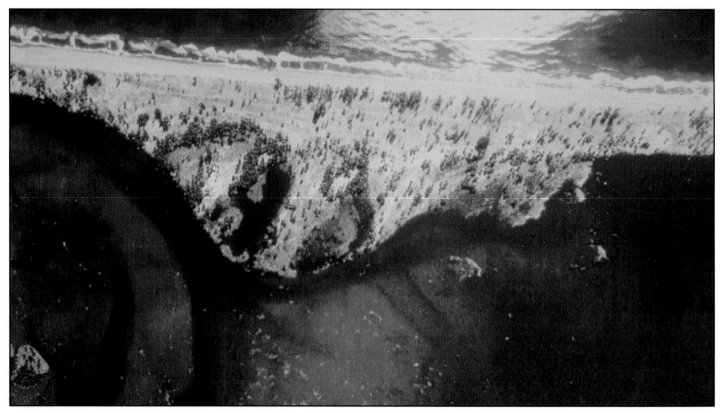

Air photo of the Sissano Lagoon spit near the lagoon mouth.

The tsunami caused extensive erosion on the back side of the spit.

1998

An offshore quake triggered a wave that struck the north coast of Papua New Guinea, killing some 2,200 people and leaving thousands more homeless. The 7.1-magnitude earthquake 24 kilometers offshore on July 17 was followed within 11 minutes by a tsunami about 12 meters tall. While the magnitude of the quake was not large enough to create these waves directly, it is believed the earthquake generated an undersea landslide, which in turn caused the tsunami.

A two-story wooden school building that stood near the church at Sissano Mission was carried 65 m by the wave until caught by a grove of coconut palms.

2004

The most powerful earthquake in 40 years triggered waves that travelled thousands of miles to crash onto the coastlines of at least five Asian countries, devastating vast areas and disastrously affecting millions of people. The 'Indian Ocean Earthquake' launched a series of lethal tsunamis on December 26, killing more than a quarter of a million people — making it the deadliest tsunami in recorded history. The death toll was heaviest in the immediate vicinity of the quake: in Indonesia, Thailand and the north-western coast of Malaysia. But it also caused fatalities thousands of kilometers away in Bangladesh, India, Sri Lanka, the Maldives, and even as far as Somalia, Kenya and Tanzania in Eastern Africa.

Below: *May, 18, 2004. Satelite image showing Meluaboh, Indonesia, before the Boxing Day Tsunami. Image courtesy Digital Globe.*

Right: *January, 7, 2005. Satelite image showing destruction of Meluaboh, Indonesia. Image courtesy Digital Globe.*

THE TSUNAMI STRIKES: TIMETABLE TO TERROR

It was a little over one minute to eight on the morning of December 26, 2004, that a magnitude 9.3 earthquake ripped apart the seafloor off the coast of north west Sumatra. More than 100 years of accumulated stress was released as a monstrous sea claw travelled thousands of kilometers across the Indian Ocean wreaking havoc in countries as far apart as Indonesia, the Maldives, Sri Lanka and Somalia. The millions of people living, fishing and vacationing around the Bay of Bengal and on the coast of Thailand and Malaysia were hundreds of miles away from the epicenter of the Tsunami. How could they know that the gentle shaking that caused skyscrapers in Singapore and Chiang Mai in northern Thailand to sway would unleash a devastating wall of water crashing onto their shore.

That Sunday when the world seemed to explode can be recaptured in this dramatic timetable as the world tried to make sense of the impending cataclysm...

11.59 pm GMT (7:59 am local time): The huge earthquake erupts in the Indian Ocean off Sumatra, Indonesia.

1.07 am GMT: Seismic signals from stations in Australia alert the NOAA Pacific Tsunami Warning Center in Hawaii about an earthquake.

1:14 am GMT: The Tsunami Warning Center in Hawaii sends a bulletin to nations that participate in the Tsunami Warning System in the Pacific (ITSU). India, Sri Lanka and the Maldives are not members of the system.

2:04 am GMT: A second bulletin is sent, alerting nations that the earthquake had a preliminary magnitude of 8.5. The bulletin says the ITSU nations do not face the threat of a tsunami, but cite the possibility of a tsunami near the quake's epicenter.

2:30 am GMT: The Warning Center alerts the Australia Management System.

3:30 am GMT: The center receives the first indications that a devastating tsunami has formed from Internet news reports of casualties in Sri Lanka. It is believed that, by that time, the deadly waves have struck the whole region.

3:45 am GMT: A Sri Lanka navy commander calls the Tsunami Center to ask about the potential for further tsunami damage and earthquake aftershocks.

4 am GMT: The US ambassador to Sri Lanka calls the Tsunami Center to set up a notification system in case of aftershocks. He says he will contact Sri Lanka's Prime Minister for such notifications. News outlets continue reports of increasing, widespread casualties.

5:45 am GMT: After the Harvard University Seismology Department revises the magnitude of the earthquake to 8.9, the Tsunami Center advises the Australian Bureau of Meteorology that the waves could hit Australia's west coasts.

6 am GMT: The center tells the U.S. Pacific Command in Hawaii about the growing earthquake magnitude and the potential for devastating tsunamis in the western Indian Ocean.

6:15 am GMT: The Australia Bureau of Meteorologists tells the Tsunami Center that it had sent out an alert concerning Australia's west coast.

8:15 am GMT: The center alerts U.S. State Department Operations to the potential threat to Madagascar and Africa.

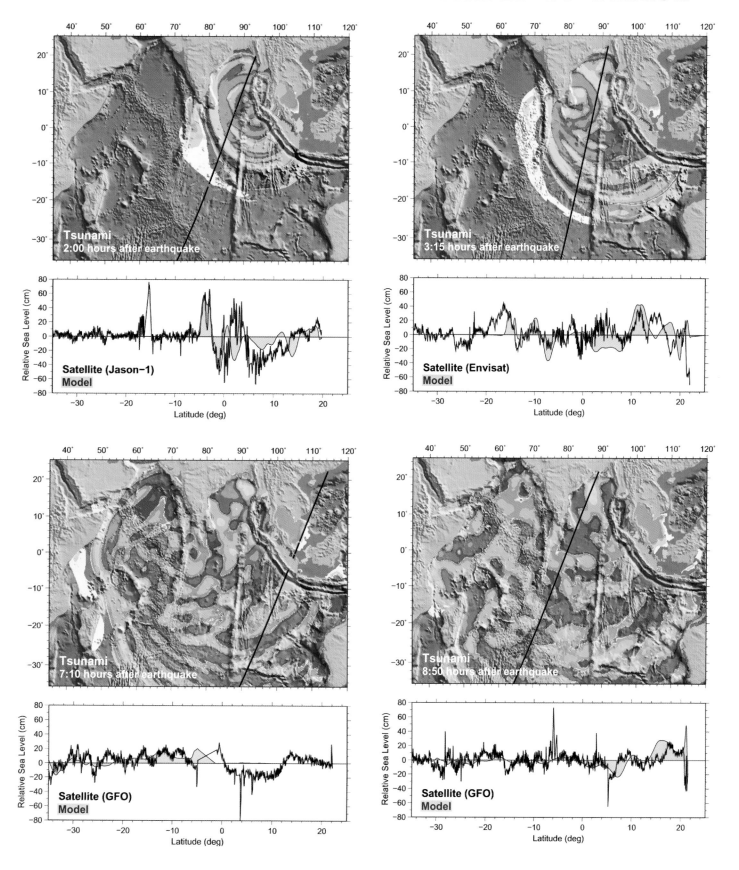

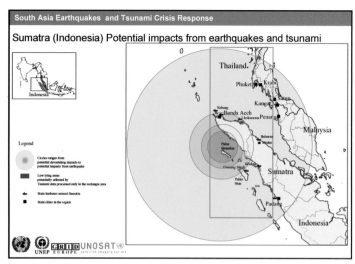

Above: *Graph showing potential earthquake zones.*

Below: *Tsunami wave field in the bay of Bengal.*

THE EARTHQUAKE

Two hundred and forty kilometers (150 miles) off the coast of Sumatra, deep under the ocean floor at the boundary between two of Planet Earth's tectonic plates, lies a 1,200 kilometer (745 miles) trench called the Andaman-Sumatran subduction zone. At about the same speed as your fingernails grow, the lower plate, carrying India, is being forced or subjected beneath the upper plate, which carries most of South East Asia — dragging it down, causing huge stresses to build up. These stresses were released that morning. The shakes from this mega-thrust went on for eight minutes and woke people from their slumbers as far away as Thailand and the Maldives.

The shaking finally subsided but no-one had any idea that the tremors had set in motion something far more deadly...

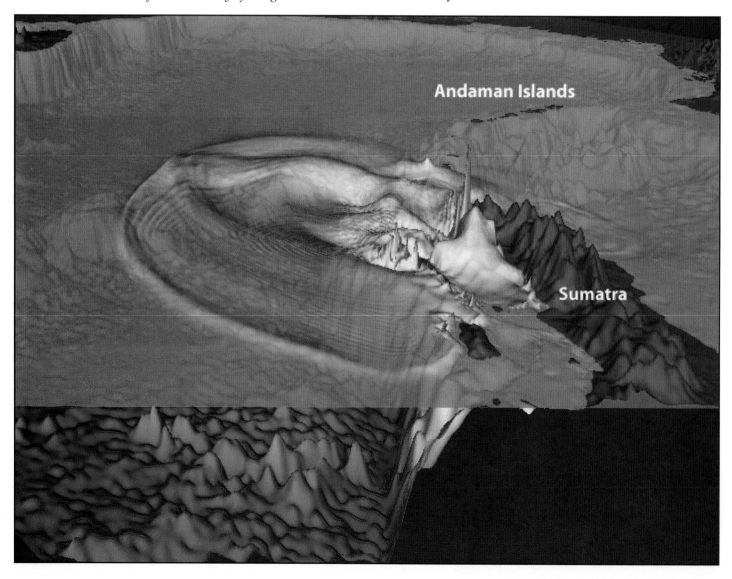

THE TSUNAMI

Deep under the Indian Ocean, at the epicenter of the quake, the 20 meter (65 feet) upward thrust of the seafloor set in motion a series of geological events. Billions of tonnes of seawater, forced upward by the movement of the seabed, now flowed away from the fault in a series of giant waves. Their total energy was equivalent to about five megatons of TNT (20 petajoules) — more than twice the explosive energy used in all of World War II, including the two atomic bombs.

The only people to have any idea what had happened were thousands of miles away in Hawaii. But, relying on seismic data alone, the scientists at the Pacific Tsunami Warning Center had no idea the earthquake had unleased an ocean-wide tsunami. As is evident from the timetable above, it was a full 50 minutes after they first picked up the tremors that they issued a warning of a possible local tsunami.

Thirty minutes after the shaking subsided, the first wave, travelling eastwards, crashed into Sumatra.

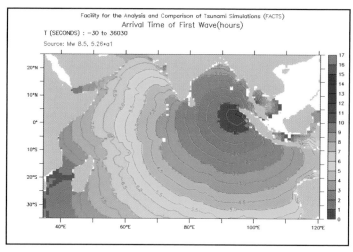

Above: *Graph showing the arrival times of waves from the epicenter of the quake.*

Below: *The maps below are computer simulations of how much the Earth moved as a result of the quake. The black star marks the epicenter. Areas marked in red yellow and green show areas that rose during the earthquake, and blue where they dropped (Left map). The right map shows the horizontal motion. The greatest motion on the sea floor was 36 feet, the coast of Sumatra moved as much as 9.8 feet.*

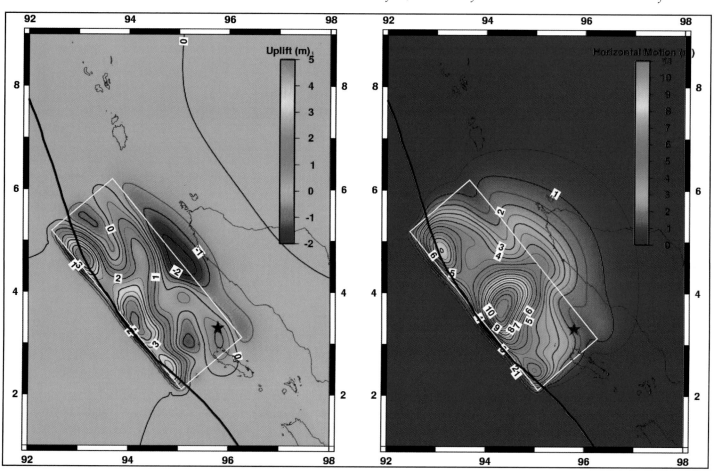

THE TRAGEDY

None of this captures the true terror and tragedy of course. While messages were being relayed, reports compiled and analysis being made, people were dying, swept away as if tiny pieces of flotsam and jetsam.

On the shores directly facing the epicenter, the waves reached heights of 20 meters, stripping vegetation from mountainsides, capsizing freighters and throwing boats into trees. Moments after Sumatra's most prominent shores were hit, its city of Banda Aceh, just a few miles round the coast, was completely destroyed. Within just 15 minutes, as many as 200,000 people had been killed.

Mohammed Firdus, 36, a telephone operator from Bireuen, Aceh province, was sitting on the porch of his house, about 200 meters from the sea when the earthquake struck. Then he heard a rumbling. Someone came running along the beach shouting "huge wave, huge wave". Said Mr Firdus: "And then I saw the water. It was wall at least a meter high coming down the track towards us all. We all immediately turned and ran towards the main road with water following us."

Ten thousand people on Nias fled to higher ground. In Aceh province, worst hit by the Tsunami, roads quickly became blocked as those with cars tried to drive as far inland as they could.

The authorities said it was impossible to judge how many people were killed by the earthquake because it was so quickly followed by the Tsunami striking Aceh province and the smaller islands such as the popular surfing resort of Nias, where an entire hotel, the Wismata Indah, was washed out to sea.

Another group of islands were equally devastated. The Andaman and Nicobar Islands are Indian owned but located close to the northern coast of Sumatra.

In areas close to the epicenter of the earthquake, land masses actually changed shape. This is what happened in the low lying archipelago of Andaman and Nicobar, made up of islands that had no natural defences in the path of the giant wave that crashed onto their shores. Villages were pounded by the waves and completely flattened, the salt water contaminating freshwater sources and destroying most of the arable land. The Tsunami reached a height of 15 meters in the southern Nicobar Islands.

The Great Nicobar and Car Nicobar islands were

the worst hit among all the islands because of their proximity to the quake and relative flatness. Among the casualties in Car Nicobar were 100 Indian Air Force personnel and their family members who were washed away when the wave hit their air base. The cathedral, one of the oldest in the region, was completely washed away. Aftershocks continued to rock the area days after the Tsunami hit the area.

Of the Andaman and Nicobar group's 572 islands, only 38 are inhabited, both by people from the mainland and indigenous tribes. The natives of the islands are endangered tribal groups, such as such as the Jarawa, the Sentinelese, the Shompen, the Onge and the Andamanese. They are some of the world's

Photos taken in Phuket, Thailand, showing waters receding before the tsunami arrives.

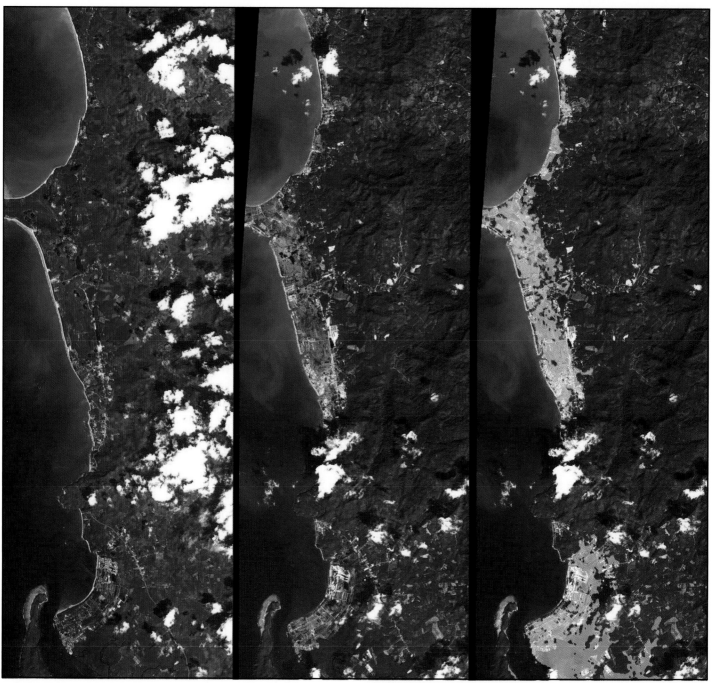

Above: *False colour enhanced, satellite image showing the devastating effects of the tsunami hitting Southern Thailand.*

"I am all right Papa, Mom. Please come back again."

Meghna Rajshekhar, child found clinging to a wooden plank at Nicobar Island.

NATURE'S WARNING SYSTEM

They seemed to sense it was coming. A herd of elephants in Thailand began behaving strangely. They stamped the ground and tugged at their chains until their mighty strength freed them and they could run higher into the hills.

At that same time, in the Thai resort of Phuket, a four-year-old elephant called Ning Nong was giving a tourist ride to and eight-year-old British girl, Amber Mason, of Milton Keynes, Buckinghamshire. Suddenly, a sixth sense made Ning Nong bolt from the beach up to higher ground. "I think Ning Nong knew something was wrong and was trying to get off the beach," said Amber. Her mother, who in the confusion thought her little girl had drowned, later said: "If she had stayed on the beach, she would never have lived..."

Elephants in Khao Lak, the hardest-hit area of Thailand, trumpeted in fear three hours before the earthquake struck hundreds of miles away. They sounded the alarm again before the deadly wave hit.

It is believed that elephants, already one of nature's most sensitive beasts, have special bones in their feet that enable them to sense seismic vibrations long before humans.

Meanwhile, off the coast of Thailand, professional diver Chris Cruz was leading an expedition when scores of dolphins erupted from the water, surrounded his boat and led him further out to sea, where he could ride the wave harmlessly rather than be swamped by it. "If we had stayed where we were, we would not have survived," he said later.

But there were more animal-instinct phenomena. Flamingos abandoned their low-lying breeding areas in Thailand. At the fishing village of San Suk, birds started squawking frantically. Villagers took heed and ran and all 1,000 escaped unharmed.

A lighthouse lookout reported seeing a herd of antelope at a wildlife sanctuary in southern India stampeding from the shoreline to nearby hills just moments before the massive waves crashed across the shore. And at Malaysia's national zoo, animals could feel imminent danger in the air and refused to come out of their pens, choosing to stay sheltered instead.

Said Richard Mackenzie, producer of a TV programme Tsunami: Animal Instinct which highlighted the unusual behaviour of animals leading up to the disaster: "This kind of behaviour was being reported in news stories at the time. But the more we looked into it, the more we realised it wasn't just a case of wild anecdotes. Eye-witness accounts by naturalists and scientists consistently showed that animals knew about the Tsunami significantly before any humans realised what was coming."

In Sri Lanka, many thousands of people were killed — but, according to staff at the national Wildlife Department, all the wild elephants and those that give rides to tourists, plus all the deer, survived. Of 2,000 animals in one sanctuary in India, only one, a boar, was killed.

Biologist Dr Mike Heithaus explained his theory on the eerie sense that animals seemed to have when the Tsunami was imminent. "Wild animals are extremely sensitive," he said. "They have excellent hearing and they probably heard the killer waves coming in the distance. There's also vibration. And there may have been changes in the air pressure which alerted animals and made them move to safer ground."

Richard Mackenzie is more succinct in his opinion of an animal's in-built 'danger radar' when a tsunami is about to hit. "Even seconds in a situation like that could without have questions have meant the difference between life and death," he said. "I guess the lesson is that we have to take more seriously and not be afraid to wonder what they're doing, why they're doing it and what they might be trying to tell us."

Tsunami waves crashing in at Patung beach, Phuket, Thailand.

most primitive tribes and considered the world's only link to an ancient civilization. Most of these tribes have maintained their aboriginal lifestyle for centuries, and government policy has been to not interfere with them unless absolutely essential. It is believed most of the native islanders survived the Tsunami because they live on higher ground or far from the coast. The Sentinelese live on a reserved island and are hostile to outsiders — which made it difficult for Indian officials to visit the island immediately after the Tsunami. The islanders shot arrows at helicopters sent to check on them.

Because this and some other isles are inhabited by groups that have little or no contact with the outside world, it was impossible to establish firm figures for the dead and injured. The official death toll was put at 812, with about 7,000 people missing. The unofficial death toll was later estimated to be all of 7,000, with 50,000 people having lost their homes. That meant that one fifth of the population of the Nicobar islands were reported dead, injured or missing.

Leaving a devastated Sumatra and its offshore islands, the waves continued across the Andaman Sea towards Thailand where the tourist resorts of Phuket and Phi Phi islands were next to be hit with a succession of tsunamis ten meters high.

Due to the complex way in which the seafloor ruptured, some waves set off travelling with the crest first, others trough first. The trough reached the shores of the west coast of Thailand, causing the sea to disappear off the beaches — one of the classic warning signs of an approaching Tsunami. Tragically, many tourists went down the beach to look, some to collect or rescue fish left flapping on the sand. A few minutes later, the first wave hit and a thousand tonnes of water crashed down on each meter of beach.

A man leading an elephant to entertain tourists when the Tsunami came put several children on the elephant's back and saved them from the flood. Waves rolled on to Patong Beach, flooded the hotel lobby in seconds and sent furniture swimming into the street. One man, 45-year-old Swede Boree Carlsson. had to wrap himself around a pillar to avoid being swept away.

At Khao Lak, the wave reached 10 meters (30 feet), causing billions of pounds of damage. One woman discovered an 18-month-old boy from Kazakhstan

Physiotherapist Debbie Boatswain, 39, from Wokingham, Berkshire, England, actually received a warning about the impending tsunami two days before it happened. She said: "I went to a palmist at my hotel in Angola on the south coast of Sri Lanka on Christmas Eve. He said to me 'Stay out of the sea — big wave'. But I took no notice."

Mrs Boatswain and her friend, 31-year-old teacher Pam Wall, moved up to the third floor of their hotel when the first swell engulfed the pool and entered the foyer of the Briton Hotel. That was just moments before the 30 feet wave struck. Said Mrs Boatswain: "People were in a total panic. It just came in within about a minute-and-a-half. People were running and screaming. It was really freaky."

Mrs Wall said they had been taking photographs of the wave as it approached, before realising its terrible force. "We thought everything was fine, then one of the waiters yelled 'This is the Day After Tomorrow', referring to the film."

floating on a mattress.

Outlying islands and tourist resorts near Phuket were also severely hit. In all, almost 8,000 people died.

A resident of Phuket, Montri Charnvichai, was on the beach at 10am when the sea first disappeared before returning with a vengeance. He said: "The first wave must have been travelling at at out 70 miles per hour. It swept up the beach, carrying everything with it."

Chris Francis, 30, from Sydney, Australia, on holiday in Phuket with his 27-year-old girlfriend Karen Tripet, described the scene in detail. "We had just come down to Patong Beach from our hotel to get some fresh air and clear our heads after heavy Christmas celebrations. The weather was perfect — clear skies with a slight breeze.

"Suddenly, we heard this loud rumbling in the distance. We looked up and saw a white-tipped wall of water bearing down on the beach. At first we just

Receding waters and beach damage from Tsunami, at Kalutara, Sri Lanka

Receding waters from Tsunami, at Kalutara, Sri Lanka.

A rural community near the coast of Sumatra lays in ruin after the Tsunami that struck South East Asia — U.S. Navy photo taken January 2, 2005 by Photographer's Mate 2nd Class Philip A. McDaniel.

"I just couldn't believe what was happening before my eyes. As I was standing there, a car actually floated into the lobby and overturned because the current was so strong. The water was up to my chest and I was holding onto my friend's hand because he can't swim."

Eye witness, Boree Carlsson from Sweden.

stayed where we were as if transfixed, not quite sure what to make of it. Then the shouting started and the screaming and the panicking. People who were in the sea rushed to get out, while those like us who were on the beach, started moving away.

"And then the first wave struck. It must have been a couple of meters high. It came crashing in, tossing boats up and throwing them around like a child's bath toys. People were screaming for help but everyone was focussing on themselves. But we didn't move fast enough because the next wave struck a few minutes later. By now, we were about 100 meters from the beach but we could hear and see the water coming after us.

"We went into a clothes shop and up to the first floor. There must have been about 20 people in there. I could see out of a window and it was a surreal sight. Cars and bikes were being swept along but so was almost everything else you could think off. It felt we

A village near the coast of Sumatra in ruin after the Tsunami struck — U.S. Navy photo by Photographer's Mate 2nd Class Philip A. McDaniel.

"And a family has just walked past carrying a very small bundle with pale white feet poking out the bottom of it. As they walked past, the teenage son, wearing an England football shirt, said in a very matter of fact way, 'My brother is dead'."

Roland Buerk, BBC correspondent, Unawatuna, Sri Lanka

stayed in the shop for hours but it was probably only about 30 minutes. When we emerged it was a scene of complete chaos and devastation."

Sakino Natoto, 27, a tour operator, was sitting just across the road from the beach when the wave crashed in. It flushed her into the basement of a store, then around and around as it carried her to the top floor.

Holidaymaker Dawn Taylor from Stockport, England, was on Kamala beach. She recalled: "It was like a really, really bad dream. It was a glorious day and a group of us were enjoying the beach when suddenly we saw this wall of water coming towards us. We just ran. The scale of devastation was just enormous."

Amongst the missing that day were Sadayuki Yoshino, the First Secretary at the Japanese Embassy in Bangkok, and his son, who were on holiday in Phuket.

The more remote Phi Phi islands, location for the movie *The Beach*, were hit even more badly than

In one of the most terrifying single incidents, around 800 people died when a train was struck by the Tsunami at Telwatta on Sri Lanka. It is believed to be the world's worst rail accident ever. Up to 1,500 people were crammed into The Queen of the Sea as it neared its destination of Galle after travelling at 75 miles an hour along the Sri Lankan coastline from Colombo. Suddenly, the waves knocked it sideways.

The force of the wave threw the train's eight cars into a bog before finally coming to rest on a hillock. The coastal railroad was left a twisted mess. The stories survivors told were chilling. This one is from 62-year-old Daya Wijaya Gunawardana, a Colombo restaurateur who was stranded in a flooded carriage, separated from his son and daughter. He spent 45 minutes trapped in the carriage before clambering out to safety.

"The train had stopped at signals. Then suddenly the sea flooded through the train, very high, very quick. The water came in about 60 feet from the sea and the whole train was filled with water. Then it fell over. I thought we were dead. But we prayed to our God and because of that I got up to a window and escaped. People were trying to escape, the whole thing was flooded so everybody tried to get out.

"I heard that out of 1,500 people, 1,000 died. When I got out of the train, there were a few wounded people, but not many. Most did not come out of the train. But my family all escaped. I have some pains ion my body. It's a narrow escape."

Outside of the train, Mr Gubnwardana was reunited with his 32-year-old son Duminda and his 31-year-old daughter Kishani. They first went to a nearby temple before moving to higher ground and trekking two miles uphill to shelter in a school.

Tourist Danny Shahaf, an Israeli living in London, recalled: "It was so quick, it washed us so far away. The carriage kept filling up with water. I was telling my friend to run to the front of the carriage, the windows there were still above the water. I pushed my friend through the window to get her up out of the carriage. There was a woman next to me holding her baby trying to hold the window open with the other hand. As I tried to help her the carriage filled completely, the water pushing the window shut. Only my friend managed to get out. Back at the other end of the carriage it was dark. I held my breath and thought 'This is how you die'."

Three days later, Buddhist monks led services for the dead, burying scores of bodies from the train. They included villagers who had scrambled aboard during a ten-minute pause in between the giant waves. A moment's silence was held in memory of the dead.

Venerable Baddegama Samitha, a monk who carried out the ritual, told Associated Press: "This was the only thing we could do. It was a desperate solution. The bodies were rotting. We gave them a decent burial."

That same day, rescuers called off the search for survivors.

Phuket. But heavy seas prevented people from being evacuated.

Dominic Stephenson and his girlfriend Eileen Lee, from Edinburgh, Scotland, were on holiday on Koh Phi Phi when waves engulfed the resort. Dominic's body was recovered allowing his family to give him a proper burial back home. Eileen's name was added to the list of those missing. Another Scot, Patricia Anthony, 44, from Rutherglen, Lanarkshire, also died in the Tsunami. She was on holiday in Phi Phi with her husband Michael and their 14-year-old son Adam, who survived by clinging to a tree.

Although Malaysia lies close to the epicenter, much of its coastline was spared widespread devastation because it was shielded by Sumatra. But still scores of people were swept from beaches on the northern island of Penang and at least 68 people were confirmed dead. Sumatra's location meant terrible death and destruction for its people, but it also saved Malaysia from a similar fate. Most of the fatalities there were children and picnickers and people swimming and jet-skiing off beaches on the island of Penang.

Above: *Homes close to the Sumatran shoreline are wrecked, and others are completely vanished — U.S. Navy photo by Photographer's Mate 2nd Class Philip A. McDaniel.*

> "It was a 30-foot wall of sea just bearing down on us like an angry monster."
> *American Dayalan Sanders, orphanage owner.*

"It was crazy. One minute I was preparing for the lunchtime rush and then the next thing I knew my tables were floating off down the street," recounted restaurant owner Lin Wei Song.

Added Canadian visitor Jasper Bintner: "At first you could just see a wall of waves in the distance with the white tops crashing down. Luckily, we had a lot of visual warning so we could get out of the water and the locals made sure we did. Around the corner, where the people were washed out to sea they didn't have any warning. The Tsunami just swept them off the beach and out to sea."

The giant waves sent parked motorcycles and cars crashing along Penang's Gurney Drive. The biggest loss from a single family was when five of Zulkifli Muhammad Noor's seven children were killed as the Tsunami struck at Pasir Panjang Beach. Other deaths were reported on the mainland in Perak and Kedah states from both tsunamis that struck and the original earthquake that destroyed thousands of buildings. Bhumi Jensen, grandson of HM King Bhumibol Adulyadej, was among those killed.

Houses in fishing villages along coastal areas were damaged in Batu Maung and Bayan Lepas in Penang coastal areas in the Peninsular Malaysia. Thirteen villages in Kuala Muda, Kedah and Kuala Triang in Langkawi island were also affected and about a quarter of holiday boats anchored in Rebak and Telafa harbour in Link were also damaged. There were no reports of deaths of foreign visitors.

Meanwhile, the westbound series of waves were heading for Sri Lanka. In the deeper waters of the Indian Ocean and barely noticeable at just 10 feet above the surface, they were travelling at 500 miles an hour. The first wave hit Sri Lanka with no 'recede' and no warning.

In all, six waves weighing over 100 billion tonnes hit Sri Lanka. It was yet another freak of nature that rocked this tiny island, instantly making it one of the Tsunami's worst victims. For as the waves rushed inland like a giant tide across the island's southern tip, they began to change direction in an affect called refraction. The part of the wave closest to the shore slowed down in the shallow wave, leaving the outer part — travelling as faster speeds — to bend around the island.

Sri Lanka's southwest coast, the side that should have been safe, was suddenly in the wave's direct

Below: *This substantial Sumatran house stands alone, although severely damaged, among the wreckage of its neighbours — U.S. Navy photo by Photographer's Mate 2nd Class Philip A. McDaniel.*

Above: *Homes and farms on higher ground survived the full effects of the Tsunami when it hit the Sumatran coast — U.S. Navy photo by Photographer's Mate 2nd Class Philip A. McDaniel*

line and cities such as Galle were destroyed, with an estimated 4,000 people losing their lives. The test match ground at Galle, where international cricket is played, was devastated.

In southern Sri Lanka, 200 prisoners escaped when the waves swept away a high-security prison in Matara. Witnesses in the eastern port city Trincomalee reported waves of 14 meters (40 feet) reaching inland as far as a kilometer (0.6 miles).

Soon, as with every other country hit by the Tsunami, reports were coming out of Sri Lanka detailing just how a monumental a tragedy it was. The BBC's Roland Buerk gave a dramatic first-hand account from Unawatuna on the south coast. He was still in bed when he heard the first sounds of of what

was to become one of our worst ever natural disasters. He reported:

"We very quickly scrambled to get out as the windows started to cave in and glass shattered everywhere. We swam out of the room neck deep in water, forcing our way through the tables and chairs in the restaurant and up into a tree. But within about 30 seconds that tree collapsed as well and we were thrust back into the water where we had to try and keep our heads above the water line. We were swept along for a few hundred meters, trying to dodge the motorcycles, refrigerators, cars and other debris that were coming with us. Then the water started coming under the door. Within a few seconds it was touching the window.

"Finally, about 300 meters inshore, we managed to get hold of a pillar, which we held onto until the waters just gradually began to subside. Other people though weren't so lucky.

Above: *An aerial view of the Tsunami-stricken coastal region near Aceh, Sumatra, Indonesia, taken on January 4, 2005 — U.S. Navy photo by Photographer's Mate 3rd Class Tyler J. Clements.*

One elderly British gentleman was walking around in a state of shock. His wife had been swimming when the waves struck."

Former German Chancellor Helmut Kohl, on vacation in Sri Lanka, was rescued from the roof of his flooded hotel by military helicopter.

As with every disaster, there were the personal stories of tragedy and triumph. Around 70 children were at their school in Mullitaivu on Sri Lanka's northern coast shortly before 9am. As the waves crashed in, the school building was flooded and the kitchen wall smashed down. While some children scaled a mango tree to evade the torrent, half the group - mostly babies and toddlers - did not make it. When the waters had gone a teacher took the babies

into her room. "They were lifeless" recalled one young survivor.

American Dayalan Sanders left Maryland in 1994 to build an orphanage – and a decade later saw it smashed to pieces. Dayalan managed to get 28 orphans and his own family into a small boat and crossed a lagoon awash with floating bodies and people begging for help. He finally reached safety in the city. When his story became public, money started rolling in to build a new orphanage.

In all, both the southern and eastern coastlines were ravaged: homes, crops and fishing boats were destroyed, and at least 400,000 people lost their jobs. Sri Lanka's agricultural land was badly, hit with paddy fields destroyed in the northern, eastern, southern and western coastal belt. Also destroyed or washed away were a large number of agricultural vehicles and equipment. Apart from homes, many hotels were also damaged. Hotels along the south

THE TSUNAMI STRIKES: TIMETABLE TO TERROR

coast were full of both foreign tourists and Sri Lankans making use of the long Christmas weekend. Canals and drains were blocked and water sources contaminated.

The science-fiction author and scuba diver, Sir Arthur C. Clarke, who lives in the capital, Colombo, was able to report that his family and staff were safe although "some are badly shaken and relate harrowing first-hand accounts of what happened." Sir Arthur's diving school, Underwater Safaris at Hikkaduwa, was destroyed.

After smashing Sri Lanka, The waves carried on further north to India, killing at least 10,000 people. Its south-east coast, especially the state of Tamil Nadu, was the worst affected area on the mainland and suffered the greatest number of dead.

In the Nagapattinam district, entire villages were instantly destroyed. At least 5,500 people were killed there, the death toll at Velankanni alone being 1,500.

Many of the victims had been visiting the Basilica of the Virgin Mary for Christmas. A nuclear power station at Kalpakkam was shut down after sea water rushed into a pump station. About 100 casualties were reported from Kalpakkam, all power plant personnel and their families.

In one state alone, Andra Pradesh, 2,000 fishing boats were lost. The fishermen along the southern coast of Coromandel had just brought in the night's catch when the Tsunami struck. Kalai Arasan in Kalapet, near Pondicherry, was crouched on the beach when he saw the ocean rise up before him. He said: "Suddenly, I heard people from the village shouting, 'Run, run for you lives'."

As the ocean raced inland, 30-year-old Mr Arasan

Below: *An aerial view of Tsunami-stricken Meulaboh, Sumatra, Indonesia, taken on January 6, 2005 — U.S. Navy photo by Photographer's Mate Airman Jordon R. Beesley.*

Previous page: *A Lone mosque stands among the damage of a coastal village near Aceh, Sumatra, Indonesia. U.S. Navy photo by Photographer's Mate 3rd Class Jacob J. Kirk.*

Right top: *An aerial view of the village of BanTuan, south of Banda Aceh in Sumatra, Indonesia. U.S. Navy photo by Photographer's Mate 2nd Class Philip A. McDaniel.*

Right bottom: *Banda Aceh, Sumatra, Indonesia pictured on January 9, 2005 – A truck still covered in water, near a downtown medical complex, from the Tsunami that hit the region — U.S. Navy photo by Photographer's Mate 1st Class Alan D. Monyelle.*

Below: *An aerial view of two ships that were washed ashore at the waterfront of an industrial area near Banda Aceh, Sumatra, Indonesia. U.S. Navy photo by Photographer's Mate Airman Jordon R. Beesley.*

Above: *On January 10, debris still litters the city of Meulaboh on the island of Sumatra, Indonesia. Meulaboh was the site of the first Landing Craft Air Cushion (LCAC) landing of Operation Unified Assistance. U.S. Marine Corps photo by Pfc. Nicholas T. Howes.*

Left: *The coast of Sumatra, Indonesia in the southern Aceh region reveals her beauty in spite of the devastation that was left in wake of the Tsunami that struck the entire region. U.S. Navy photo by Photographer's Mate 3rd Class M. Jeremie Yoder.*

Next page: *Picking through the ruins of Meulaboh on the island of Sumatra, this picture taken January 10. U.S. Navy photo by Photographer's Mate 3rd Class Jennifer Rivera.*

clung to a coconut palm near his village at Kanaga Chettkuluan, one of the worst hit areas along the coastline south of Madras. He was not to know until later that although his wife had climbed to safety on a roof, his daughters Dhia, 13 and Desika, just 20 days old, were swept away to their deaths.

In just a few minutes, 1,800 villagers were killed along the eastern Indian coastline and thousands more were left homeless.

Because the quake's 1,200 kilometers of faultline ran roughly north to south, the greatest strength of the Tsunami waves was to the east and west. Bangladesh, lying at the northern end of the Bay of Bengal, had few casualties despite being a low-lying country relatively close to the epicenter.

Directly in line to the west, however, was one of the lowest lying countries on Earth, The Maldives, consisting of 199 inhabited islands. It was the islands' unique geography that saved them all from near obliteration. Being just tips of underwater volcanoes and without a continental shelf to push the wave

height up, the Tsunami just washed through. Coral reefs, acting like a giant colander, may also have given protection by stripping the waves of energy. But still 20 islands were totally destroyed. Miraculously, the death toll was less than 100.

As the waves left the Maldives, they passed through a narrow gap between the island chains, focusing their energy directly at Somali - the worst-hit African state. Damage was concentrated in the region of Puntland, on the tip of the Horn of Africa. The water destroyed 1,180 homes, smashed 2,400 boats and rendered freshwater wells and reservoirs unusable. Around 300 people died, thousands were left homeless, and as many as 30,000 people displaced.

THE TSUNAMI STRIKES: TIMETABLE TO TERROR

Left: *Roland Koopman, a volunteer from the Netherlands walks among the ruins of a house near the village of Hikkaduwa southern Sri Lanka, on January 13, 2005.*

Below: *A Sri Lankan man walks by a statue of Buddha laying among the ruins of a collapsed temple on the coast road near the village of Hikkaduwa, southern Sri Lanka, on January 13.*

Previous page: *Banda Aceh, Sumatra, Indonesia (Jan. 15 2005) - Military and commercial support ships operate relief efforts just off-shore from the devastation of downtown Banda Aceh. U.S. Navy photo by Photographers Mate Third Class Benjamin D. Glass.*

Right top: *Region of Glebruk, Sumatra, Indonesia (Jan. 17, 2005) - A house lies nearly on its side in one of the coastal towns hit by the Tsunami — U.S. Navy photo by Photographer's Mate 2nd Class Elizabeth A. Edwards.*

Right bottom: *A small valley in the region of Glebruk on the island of Sumatra, lies in ruins — U.S. Navy photo by Photographer's Mate 2nd Class Elizabeth A. Edwards.*

Below: *Banda Aceh, Sumatra, Indonesia (Jan. 17, 2005) – A large boat sits among the rubble in Banda Aceh — U.S. Navy photo by Photographer's Mate 3rd Class Katrina V. Walter.*

Next page: *An aerial shot taken on January 18, of tsunami-damaged fishing boats at a fishing hamlet in Nagapattinam, in the southern Indian state of Tamil Nadu.*

The death toll of fishermen was never officially known.

In Burma, the worst affected area was the Irrawaddy Delta, inhabited by poor subsistence farmers and fishing families. The country's military junta put the death toll at 61, but the World Food Programme said this total was probably an underestimate.

By the time it hit Tanzania, the mighty strength of the Tsunami was sapping. It killed ten people there. By the time it reached Kenya, its waves were diminished, their force slightly dissipated by the height of the ocean bed around the Seychelles and Diego Garcia. Only one fatality was reported in Kenya, the warning system having finally had an effect and beaches having been evacuated. That solitary victim died after being drowned in the ebbing wave — the last immediate victim of one of the world's greatest natural disasters.

But many thousands of people were still not accounted for...

Previous page: *Aerial view of Banda Aceh, Sumatra, on January 19, three weeks after a Tsunami devastated the coastal region. U.S. Navy photo by Photographer's Mate 1st Class John D. Yoder.*

Above: *On February 12, 2005, six weeks after the tsunami hit Banda Aceh, it is still difficult to tell where the sea stops and land begins. U.S. Navy photo By Photographer's Mate 1st Class Jon Gesch.*

Right: *The Military Sealift Command (MSC) hospital ship USNS Mercy (T-AH 19) cruises off the coast of Banda Aceh. U.S. Navy photo by Photographer's Mate 1st Class Jon Gesch.*

THE TSUNAMI STRIKES: TIMETABLE TO TERROR

This spread: *Four photos from Khao Lak, Thailand, after the devastating Tsunami.*

Next spread: *Photograph showing the Tsunami hitting a holiday resort in Phuket, Thailand.*

Previous page: *An aerial shot of Kolhufushi island in the Maldives taken on January 10, 2005.*

Right top: *Two Sri Lankans work on rebuilding their house near the wreckage of a tsunami-hit train in Peraliya, southern Sri Lanka, on February 21, 2005.*

Right bottom: *Acehnese boys search for belongings in water in the tsunami-devastated city of Banda Aceh on the Indonesian island of Sumatra, on January 29.*

Below: *An aerial view of the city of Banda Aceh, damaged by the quake-triggered Tsunami, on the Indonesian island of Sumatra taken on January 24, 2005.*

Next page: *The sun rises over Baiturrahman mosque and the tsunami-damaged houses in Banda Aceh on January 26.*

MIRACULOUS SURVIVAL

As with any disaster, there were the stories of those who somehow made it against all the odds. Like the 70 divers, many of them foreign tourists, who were plucked to safety as at least two tsunami waves stuck Thailand's famous Emerald Cave they were exploring.

Sometimes, these tales were nothing short of miraculous, as was the case of Swedish baby, 18-month-old Hannes Bergstrom. Ron Rubin and Rebecca Beddall from Seattle, Washington, spotted the little boy wrapped in blankets on high ground, after climbing onto the roof of their Phuket hotel to escape the flood. They took him to a local hospital to join the throng of those who had been separated from their families.

A photo of Hannes taken after his rescue was posted on the internet, where it was spotted by relatives. One, Viola Hell Stroem, the little boy's aunt, said that although his face was scratched and mosquito-bitten, she recognised him straight away. "I screamed for joy. We thought he was dead," she told a newspaper in Sweden. The child's father and grandfather were tracked down to another hospital in Thailand and all three had a joyous reunion. The

"I can remember the white foam, how the surf took them up and they disappeared. I could hear people shouting at me 'Get off the beach' as I ran past them but I ignored them. I had to try to save my children. Nothing was going to stop me."
Swedish policewoman Karin Svaerd

Photo showing Karin Svaerd rushing to save her children from the oncoming tsunami wave.

MIRACULOUS SURVIVAL

Karin Svaerd relaxing with her family back in Sweden after her ordeal with the Tsunami.

reunion was happy too for Ms Beddall: "He had a toy and he kept squeezing it and he was talking. When we had him, he was not playing and he was not talking. So it made us very happy to see him normal again." Sadly, the child's mother was one of 1,500 Swedes reported missing after the tragedy.

A 23-year-old Indonesian man, Rizal Shahputra, survived by floating on the branches of a tree in the Indian Ocean for an incredible eight days and living off rainwater and coconuts which he cracked open with a doorknob he had found. Mr Shahputra had been cleaning a mosque in Banda Aceh on the northern tip of Sumatra when he was swept out to sea with a host of others including members of his family. But one by one, they had all died, leaving him to fight the greatest battle of his life. He later told reporters: "At first there were some friends with me. After a few days they were gone. I saw bodies left and right." At least one ship sailed past Mr Shahputra without noticing him before a container vessel, the *MV Curban Bridge*, spotted him 100 miles from Banda Aceh.

Acehnese man Ari Afrizal was rescued two weeks after the Tsunami destroyed his home town. He lived on makeshift rafts and a leaky fishing boat until being spotted by an Arab container. Mr Afrizal was building a house with friends in the Aceh town of Calang when the tsunami struck. Caught up in the wave, he was first pushed and then sucked out to see when the waters receded. For 24 hours, he clung to a log before managing to climb inside a damaged wooden boat and then constructing a raft made from debris. Mr Afrizal, who survived on coconuts for the first 12 days, then found all food supplies had dried up and said he had given up all hope of being rescued. Passing ships had not noticed him - until one saw his desperate waving."I managed to whistle at the ship and then waved my hands," said Mr Afrizal. "The ship sped on but it sounded the klaxon and I stood up. I thought the ship had left the area and I sat down and cried. But then it returned for me."

One visitor to Thailand, 37-year-old Swedish policewoman Karin Svaerd, survived by hanging on to a palm tree. The ten minutes it took for her to discover that her husband Lars, her sons Anton, 14

Left: *The Tsunami wave speeds through a hotel complex in Southern Koh Lanta, Thailand.*

Above: *The Tsunami swamps the grounds of a hotel on the beach at Phuket, Thailand.*

and Filip, 11, and her brother Per, had also survived, seemed an eternity. Back home in Sweden, Mrs Svaerd said: "Now our family is closer than every before. We cam so close to death that we realise how valuable life is."

French firefighters on Sumatra managed to save 25-year-old Jansen Silalalahi, found three days after the tsunami pinned him between a motorbike and a cupboard.

One man was trapped for almost five days under rubble on the Indonesian island of Nias. Hendra, 42, was pulled out alive after Singaporean rescue workers and Indonesian soldiers dug for seven hours through the concrete walls of his home and motorbike shop in Gunung Sitoli. Hendra's brother Junianto, who alerted rescuers after hearing him cry for water, fell to his knees and thanked everyone who had been involved in saving his brother. "I never believed

he had died, even though many people told me he had," he said. Rescue worker Omar Flores, described Hendra's survival as "a miracle".

At least eleven foreign tourists who had also been missing for three days were found alive on Nias. A search helicopter found the survivors — two Swedes, two French, one US national, one German, three Britons and two Canadians — in a surfing resort.

But perhaps the most astonishing survival story is that of a young woman who said she lived on wild fruits for 45 days after tsunami waves ravaged the Andaman Islands. The 18-year-old woman was rescued from Pillopanja, one of the southernmost islands of the archipelago, according to the police chief of nearby Campbell Bay island. He identified the distraught woman only as 'Jessy' and said her husband and her one-year-old child were missing, presumed dead.

MIRACULOUS SURVIVAL

Left top: *Thai tsunami survivors perform their daily activities at a temporary camp, in the Thai town of Or-Bo-Tor.*

Left bottom: *Two hotel employees (orange shirt and blue shirt, center), have just returned three-and-a-half-year old Esther to her family, who were staying at the Hotel Club Lanka. The employees grabbed the youngster when the tsunami hit and ran to a hospital four miles away. Courtesy of William Recktenwald, Southern Illinois University Carbondale.*

Below: *Esther (blond child, rear of the photo) is held by her older sister as 35 foreign hotel guests are evacuated on a flatbed truck. Courtesy of William Recktenwald, Southern Illinois University Carbondale.*

THE MISSING ONES

When the extent of the Tsunami became clear, shock followed by terrible sadness hit those who had loved ones in the disaster-stricken countries.

Parents, relatives and friends flew half way round the world to try to discover the whereabouts of people who were lost — found neither dead nor alive in the mayhem of those early days. Photographs of the missing, together with their descriptions and telephone numbers to ring with any news, were posted up at makeshift help centres throughout areas hit by the tsunami. No-one who saw the images of weeping relatives or survivors beside pictures of a smiling face will ever forget them.

Sweden, the country that suffered one of the highest number of foreign fatalities, initially also reported one of the highest number of its people missing. As of January 3, 2005, more than 2,900 Swedes were unaccounted for in the tragedy. So too were 1,100 South Africans and 1,000 Germans.

By January 12, 2005, authorities in the USA had received 4,759 inquiries about Americans missing in Southern Asia. At that time, there were 3,500 cases that had not been resolved. In all, the State Department received approximately 24,000 inquiries about loved ones or acquaintances who may or may not be in the region, or inquiries about areas affected by the tsunami. A total of 20 Americans are missing, presumed dead.

By January 6 2005, State Department deputy spokesman Adam Ereli said US authorities had answered all but 2,500 of the 24,000 inquiries about missing Americans. By comparison, the list of missing after the September 11th terrorist attacks peaked at nearly 7,000, and was eventually reduced to 3,016.

Below: *A tsunami survivor looks for her missing relatives among the photographs of unidentified victims in Velankanni, 365 km (219 miles) south of the Indian city of Madras.*

Reuniting people was an almost impossible task. But not as impossible as trying to ascertain just how many people were missing, either by some miracle, swept away to safety, or more likely, to their deaths. Those who had friends and family in the tsunami clung to hope as fiercely as many of them had clung to each other when the killer wave hit.

Emergency and hospital telephone lines were blocked constantly with people desperately seeking information. But it was an opportunity for new technology to work some magic. As many as 400 sites on the internet were set up for people to post pleas for information on those missing or — with a little help from God — for those who could announce "I'm alive!"

By the desperate nature of the appeals for information, it soon became clear that the whereabouts of many those missing or the true number lost without trace would never be known. Some sites warned of "extremely graphic" images of the deceased.

One site set up in Thailand was devised by volunteer programmers and web-site developers. It aimed to put all data available on the dead and missing in one place, instead of forcing people to surf the huge number of other sites. In a round-the-clock operation, volunteers in Phuket entered data from forms filled out by those looking for people at hospitals and Buddhist temples being used as temporary morgues.

At one time, they had data on about 4,900 people listed as dead, missing and injured. Photos of unidentified bodies, bloated and decomposing, were posted on the site in the hope clothing or jewellery or other personal items pictured with the bodies could be used to identify them. People could also submit missing-persons forms online. Chitcharen Vesespadthaya, a businessman who is managing the web site, said: "Once the body is identified, we take the picture out; we want to respect the families."

Major charities, of course, became involved in the search for survivors, with such groups as the Red Cross acting as clearing houses. Prestigious media companies like the UK's BBC and America's CNN also had message boards and information sites. And every individual country affected had its own site with lists of names of those had been tracked down or who were being sought by their families.

MISSING PERSONS

I'm currently looking for a close relative who is missing in Thailand after the tsunami struck. Her name is Francisca Cooper. She is Caucasian, blond wavy hair, 1.7 meters tall, athletic, 26 years old, Chilean, and was spending her honeymoon with her husband Mr. Aurelio Montes at the Princess Resort in Phi Phi Island. She has a small scar at the front base of her neck. Her whole family is really desperate, and we don't know if she's alive or conscious...

A group of four senior scientists from Pune, India, including Dr. Ramesh Bidwe, not traceable since the tsunami attack on 26 December from Nicobar. Kindly contact the following email address in case any information is received.

Kindly help me locate my maternal aunt SWARNALATHA H.V working for MAJITHA SCHOOL, MALE, MALDIVES, and her daughters LAKSHMI aged 22 years, PARVATHY alias JUDY, aged 20 years, and son RAGHU, aged 16 years. We have not heard from them since 26/12/2004.

Friday, January 07, 2005: Missing Children in Sri Lanka. Sachin Vimukthi, the five-year-and-seven-month-old son of Dr. W. M. Senadheera, Medical Officer at Galle Karapitiya General Hospital, has been missing since December 26. Sachin was wearing a light blue T-shirt with an elephant picture printed on it. One tooth in the upper and two in the lower had been lost at the time of his going missing at Ranliya Hotel, Hambantota. He sucks the thumb of the right arm as a habit. Any information could be given to Dr. Senadheera on 091-2246752 or 0777273131. Informant will be rewarded.

Eight-year-old Hiruni Tharushika Wanniarachchi has been missing since December 26, the day the Tsunami hit coastal areas. She was travelling with her parents in the Galle-bound train at the time of the disaster. Her father Nihal Wanniarachchi seeks public support to find the girl. Contact Nihal on 011-2515961 if you have any information.

This one-and-a-half-year-old boy went missing while he was at Ranliya Hotel in Hambantota at the time the tsunami devastated the area. As the boy is unable to speak, circulating this message may help locate him quickly.

Missing Family in Sri Lanka: Denis Caromel is searching for the rest of his family. Now in France after a week-long stay in a Colombo, Sri Lanka, hospital, he was separated from his wife and two children when they were staying at the Yala Safari Beach Hotel, half a kilometer from the entrance of the Yala National Park in Sri Lanka when the tidal wave reached the area. They were in their room at the hotel.

I am searching for my friend, Dewi Safitri, from Indonesia. Her birthdate: 21st Oct. 1973. We had thought her safe but this week received a message from her brother Rey and sister Aman that she was in Aceh, and is now missing. The last postal address I have for her was her brother's in Yogyakarta, so we have no way of knowing exactly where she was at the time of the earthquake and tsunami.

Saturday, January 01, 2005: MISSING — Melanie Clough, aged 46, a British woman, has been reported missing from Khao Lak Beach, Phuket, Thailand.

Melanie is 46 years old, has blonde hair, blue eyes and is 5ft 10 (1.77 meters). She may be identified by a breast scar due to mastectomy and reconstructive surgery. She was last seen wearing purple shorts, a white T-shirt and could have a pink or blue swimming suit underneath her clothes.

I am Looking for John Jones, originally of Cwmbran, South Wales, UK, travelling alone somewhere in Thailand. I last heard from him on Xmas day. Have not heard since. From his sister Diane Guilfoyle.

BILL (Stockport, England) & WONTONA DAVIES (Thai), somewhere in Thailand — we are desperate to hear news from you. Please be well.

Posted on one of the missing person's sites was a message from the family of young biologist Ambika Prasanna Tripathy, from Cuttack, in Orissa, who was

Below: *Pictures of survivors from Khao Lak*

Every tragedy has one story which haunts. And in the 2004 Tsunami, it was the case of a tiny child who became known worldwide as Baby No 81.

The baby boy was so-called because he was the 81st patient to be admitted to a hospital in the eastern town of Kalmunai, Sri Lanka, on the day of the tsunami. At first his identity was unknown. So too was his real age. But, as one American journalist wrote: "Baby No. 81's awful burden is not in being unwanted, but in being wanted too much." For once the news broke that a baby boy had been found alive, nine couples came forward to claim he was their son. It could have been the enormity of the emotion at time.

It could have been an unthinking bid to replace what they knew they had lost. It could have been total desperation. One will never know. But their faces, together with that of the obviously traumatised child, were flashed across the world in the midst of the horror that was the Boxing Day tsunami of 2004. Baby No 81 became Sri Lanka's most celebrated orphan.

Several of those claiming the child as theirs threatened to commit suicide if he was not given to them. Amongst all this turmoil, countless other parents who had lost their babies arrived at the hospital to see if, by some miracle, this was him. The hospital was mobbed and the child was hidden in an operating theatre each night for his own protection.

This hysteria might be easier to understand when one learns that, according to UNICEF reports, four out of every dead in Sri Lanka were children - and many of them were babies.

Said Dr. K. Muhunthan, the hospital gynaecologist who took on Baby No. 81's case: "Most of them believe this is their baby. Maybe all children they look at, they think it's their baby. I'm not angry at them really."

Judge M P Moahaiden, the Kalmunai magistrate handling the claim for parentage, added: "All the people of this community are affected, physically and psychologically. They don't know what they are doing. In the meantime, the court has to do the right thing."

On February 14, following DNA testing, the court ruled that Jeyaraja Junitha, aged 25, and her husband Murugpillai, 30, were his parents. Mrs Junitha had always known it. During one of her many visits to the hospital, she had touched his head and talked about a birthmark. "I know the shape of his ear; I can recognize my son." she said of her only child.

The stricken mother also explained that the four-month-old child - real name Abilash - was in her sister's arms when the tsunami hit. Her sister was found tangled in a tree, but safe. The baby was missing. Relatives had even counselled Jayaraja to accept his death. Now she could not hide her joy.

Dr. K. Muhunthan, meanwhile, carried on with just one of the tasks he had to undertake - photographing all the dead babies arriving at his hospital and passing the pictures to the police.

Only a handful of stranded babies in Sri Lanka did not have relatives to care for them. According to UNICEF, of the 981 children who were left with no parents, 945 were taken in by extended family. Anxious about trafficking, Sri Lanka instituted a temporary ban on the adoption of tsunami orphans.

working on a Leatherback sea turtles project near Campbell Bay in Great Nicobar. The message read:

The last time he had talked to his family was a week before the Tsunami struck the island. "We don't have any information about him," said Pratibha Tripathy, wife.

Uncertainty looms. Tripathy was camping at Point 41 in Great Nicobar for a research project funded by the Andaman Nicobar Environment Trust (ANET). Because the area is not open to civilians and the communication lines are also dead, the family has been appealing to the Coastguard and local government agencies for information, but all in vain.

In the news, they say the tribal pockets there are alright. If that is the case, the area must also be alright and somebody should have gone and found out about the welfare of the people there, especially the outsiders," said N K Tripathy, the father.

Although Tripathy's wife and father have not lost hopes, it's been a nightmarish week-long wait for his mother. And until there is some information available on the researcher, each passing minute only adds to the family's worst apprehensions.

Above: *Canada's Foreign Minister Pierre Pettigrew looks at photographs of missing people while visiting a tsunami relief center in Phuket, Thailand, January 8, 2005.*

Right: *Acehnese residents, volunteering as 'body collectors', carry bodies to a mass grave in tsunami-ravaged town of Lhoknga on January 28, 2005.*

Next page: *Thais and foreigners gather at a stadium on January 5, for a candlelight vigil and to release floating lanterns in memory of the tsunami victims on the Thai island of Phuket.*

Left: *The bodies of thousands of victims of the Tsunami which hit the Indonesian city of Banda Aceh. Soldiers searched for bodies in treetops, families wept over the dead laid on beaches and rescuers scoured coral isles for missing tourists.*

Above: *A young Thai lights candles during a vigil for tsunami victims on Patong beach in Thailand's tropical island of Phuket, January 31, 2005.*

One website message was particularly sad...

MISSING: KRISTIAN WALKER. Last known location: Thailand. Sex: male. Age: 12. Nationality: Sweden.

A CNN report on January 6, 2005, told how it was originally believed that the 12-year-old boy had been kidnapped from a Thai hospital by a child trafficker. In those dark days after the Tsunami, this offered some hope to Kristian's family. His grandfather, Daniel Walker, who went to Thailand to search for the boy, said: "I should say I'm hoping he's been kidnapped, as opposed to having been killed initially, because, if he's been kidnapped, there's a possibility that he's alive."

But the reports later turned out to have been based on a case of mistaken identity. Kristian had never been at the hospital. Kristian was back on the missing list with the 700 or so other Swedes who vanished directly after the tsunami hit Thailand.

Idyllic holiday destination Thailand had the longest

list of missing foreigners, with names such as James W. Hsu, an American second-year MBA student, being added. James was on holiday there following a study tour and went missing in the Tsunami. His disappearance was confirmed by Robert Joss, Dean of the Graduate School of Business at Stanford University, who said: "We are doing everything possible to support the search for him and we are proud of our students who are still assisting on the ground in Thailand."

Even four months after the Tsunami, some people still had hope. Eric Riley, 35, was one of 11 Scottish people officially listed as missing or confirmed as dead. He had been working in Thailand as a DJ when the tsunami struck. Nothing was heard from him after that. But Dawn Dawes, from Perth, Scotland, still searched every possible avenue to find out what had happened to her half-brother. In an interview with the newspaper *Scotland on Sunday*, which sums up the plight of many of those still searching for news of their loved ones, Dawn said:

Above: *Sri Lankan Muslims pray before burying a tsunami victim on the beach in Kalmuni, December 30, 2004. Over 150 bodies were buried in seven mass graves on the beach.*

Right: *A worker places ice on top of bodies of tsunami victims to preserve them in Takua Pa, Phanga Nga province, in Thailand's Phuket island, January 2, 2005.*

บริษัท ต้ายเหมืองขีษู๊ดส์ อำตัด
53329
JURI MARTALER
GIELGENSTR 54

บริษัท ต้ายเหมืองขีษู๊ดส์ อำตัด

"Eric has been in Thailand for a long time. He usually comes over to the UK every once in a while but, according to the British embassy in Thailand, he was definitely in the country at the time of the tsunami. I have left messages on every website I could find after the Tsunami, but he can't get e-mail access and there's no phone contact over there, so we're just playing a waiting game.

"I have also contacted the Foreign Office, but all they said was that they would get in touch with next of kin if there was any news. So I have been on the internet and looked through the pictures of all the people caught up in the tsunami, which was really upsetting.

"Eric is quite free-spirited and is not the sort of person who would phone home every week. But he would send the occasional e-mail and phone occasionally. I would have thought that, with something like this happening, he would have been

Above: *German Svetlana Martaler of Bonn is helped by her translator to prepare the body of her husband, Juri, at a temple in Thap Lamu, Thailand, December 30, 2004.*

Right: *An Acehnese man ties a rope to a woman as he tries to rescue her while being swept by the Tsunami along a river in Banda Aceh, Sumatra, on December 26, 2004. Both victims were later swept away by the strong current and killed, according to the photographer.*

in contact, even if it was a quick e-mail, to say that he was fine. I can't understand why we haven't heard from him. But, you know, there's thousands of people still missing. We're just hoping that no news is good news."

Above: *Makeshift accomodation on a beach in Somalia following the Boxing Day Tsunami.*

Right: *Tsunami damage in Hafun, Somalia. Image courtesy of WFP/Francesco Broli.*

THE WORLD BECOMES ONE

If the century has not seen a disaster of such magnitude, then neither has it witnessed such extraordinary compassion. Individuals, businesses and governments responded within hours of the horrific images of the Tsunami being flashed around the world.

States of Emergency were declared in Sri Lanka, Indonesia, and the Maldives and the United Nations declared the relief operation would be the costliest ever. UN Secretary General Kofi Annan stated that reconstruction would probably take between five and ten years. And beyond the immediate tragedy, it was feared the final death toll would double as a result of diseases, prompting a massive humanitarian response.

In Thailand, Tuk Tuk drivers were quick to offer assistance, driving victims to hospital and higher ground and away from the surging waters. At some places in Phuket and Phang Nga provinces, elephants were used to move and lift heavy wreckage to search for victims and clear roads. These included six male Indian elephants that had previously been used in making the movie *Alexander*.

New Year's Eve 2004 was a muted affair in many parts of the world. Across the globe from London's Trafalgar Square to the beaches of Thailand, people held candlelit vigils instead of the traditional celebrations. Hotels and other public places cancelled their New Year entertainments and parties. In Malaysia, Prime Minister Datuk Seri Abdullah Ahmad Badawi cut short his holiday in Spain and instructed the government to cancel all New Year celebrations. He urged everyone to hold prayers and remembrance services instead. The government also considered postponing the deportation of illegal immigrants and extending an amnesty so that they could exit the country by January 31, 2005, instead of December 31, 2004.

The Australian Government designated Sunday January 16 as a national day of mourning in Australia with people being asked to observe a minute's silence at 11.59am.

Relief organisations went into action straight away. Oxfam flew in basic emergency supplies including tents, 25,000 food packs containing rice, flour dhal,

fish, sugar and cereal and 10,000 packs containing other essential items such as soap, candles and matches, water, body bags, fuel and basic medical supplies. More specialist equipment including 1,000-litre water pumps, water tanks and communications equipment soon followed. On the island of Simeuleu, off Sumatra, 200 tonnes of food aid alone was quickly distributed.

The Tsunami was no respecter of creed, age or profession. Soon after it hit Sumatra came reports that a number of nurses and doctors had died. Together with hospitals and surgeries hit, the very life-saving service that was crucial was rendered useless. Those doctors and nurses who were unscathed in the disaster moved into camps for the homeless, where they believed their presence would be most significant. Others, so traumatised by what they had experienced and seen, moved away from the Tsunami sites of destruction. Said one official: "Some are so traumatised that a return to work may be months away, if ever."

Humanitarian group World Vision set about improving the health of communities as well as the rebuilding of a new medical structure throughout the affected areas. Arriving in Aceh, Dr Mesfin Teklu, Health and Nutrition Manager on the Global Response Team, promised: "We're going to work through provincial health departments to support the capacity-building of health professionals, the reconstruction of health facilities and the provision of essential medical equipment as well as medicines. World Vision will contribute to the recovery and rehabilitation of worst-affected communities through targeted interventions that address key concerns, like malaria and dengue fever, which are common to this region, as well as other communicable diseases. We will engage in building and staffing of new clinics in IDP relocation sites over the next few months. As there are very few health staff remaining here, we will need to train up workers."

Meanwhile, World Vision also provided monthly food rations to 40,000 people in the city of Banda Aceh and surrounding Aceh Besar district. The distributions were carried out in co-operation with the Indonesian Red Cross and local partners. Around 5,856 people received blankets, shovels, hoes, family

"Please sir, help us, we are starving."

*Man in the Nias town of Gunung Sitoli,
watching looters at a store.*

hygiene and household kits, tents, water, high-energy biscuits, mosquito nets, mats and scarves. World Vision also provided ambulances, surgical and laboratory equipment, essential drugs and medical personnel. It set up ten temporary medical clinics with 20 health care clinics planned. It also set about building 80 Temporary Living Centres (TLCs). Said Mark Holt, Shelter Manager in Aceh: "The TLCs are a much better alternative to overcrowded tarpaulins, tents, damaged houses and other buildings where many homeless are currently living."

Collecting bodies was a gruesome and heart-rendering task for search parties equipped with body bags, gloves and boots. Said Bernt Apeland, spokesman for the International Committee of the Red Cross in Banda Aceh: "As long as they are not in direct contact with drinking water, it's not really a problem. But it's a question of human dignity to retrieve the bodies and bury them. It's a kind of closure for the relatives. It's also a basic part of the clean-up of the area." According to news reports, 14,000 bodies were buried in a mass grave on the first day of the clean-up alone.

In Sri Lanka, money was collected for those who had lost everything, and vans with public announcement systems drove around calling on people to give whatever they could spare. Even in the poorest, most remote areas, people flocked to the roadside to hand over money, clothes, bottles of water and bags of rice and lentils.

A three-ship fleet carrying 2,000 US Marines bound for Iraq, left its Diego Garcia port and headed straight to Sri Lanka. The fleet included a dozen heavy-lift helicopters and badly-needed surgical hospitals.

Within days of the tsunami hitting Sri Lanka, the first of seven airlifts of water sanitation equipment arrived at Colombo to be distributed to the nine districts where World Vision was helping survivors. Then came shipping containers holding 20,000 kitchen cooking sets, over 7,000 blankets and 1,000 tents, followed by 35,000 collapsible water containers.

As Sri Lankans tried to make sense of it all, they also worked out a rough rescue plan to try to put their country back together again. The three-point plan was first to supply water, dried food, canned fish and basic medicines and clothing; then to provide dry rations such as milk powder to those in refugee camps, and thirdly to make all efforts to prevent and treat outbreaks of disease caused by polluted water and lack of proper sanitation. That was the immediate practical plan. But officials had to admit: "In the longer term, rebuilding of life and property would take an enormous effort and would need worldwide help."

The Australian, Bangladeshi, English and South African cricket teams announced that they would make donations to the rescue effort in Sri Lanka and other Asian countries. The Indian cricket team pledged funds to the humanitarian effort in southern India and cricket teams worldwide announced two one-day matches to raise further funds.

Groups such as Sri Lanka's Autism Awareness Campaign and the Rotary Club of Colombo launched international appeals. The Rotary Club statement included: "At a time of this national disaster the nation and its people must stand together to help the million victims who have been displaced from their homes and loved ones. Not only have these people lost their families, they have lost everything except for the clothes on their backs."

Sri Lankan Prime Minister Mahinda Rajapaksa set up his own personal 'hot line' for donations. Twenty thousand soldiers were deployed in government-controlled areas to assist in relief operations and maintain law and order after sporadic looting, which prompted curfews to be introduced.

America's 33rd Rescue Squadron based at Kadena Air Base, Japan, arrived in stricken areas daily with relief supplies of hygiene kits, water, plastic sheeting and medicine and food on six helicopters. "It's a tremendous feeling to know that we play a part in helping people put their lives back together here," said one helper, Airman 1st Class Emily Starcher, an HH-60 Pave Hawk helicopter flight engineer. "I feel proud to be a part of this operation. It's a great mission. We're making a difference."

Above: *Truck full of tsunami relief supplies paid for by American students being delievered by Thai students*

Right: *The first NetReliefKit designed by Cisco Systems was made operational in early July in Banda Aceh at the offices of Save The Children and was successfully tested for voice and data communications over the internet. Two other NRK's were been deployed by Catholic Relief Services and World Vision.*

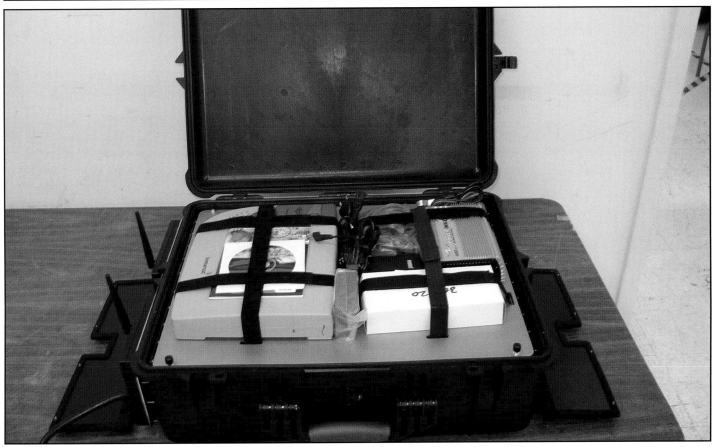

THE WORLD BECOMES ONE

Right top: *Medan, Indonesia (Jan. 4, 2005) - Marines assigned to 3rd Transportation Support Battalion, 3rd Force Service Support Group, help distribute humanitarian relief supplies at Palonia Air Field in Medan. U.S. Marine Corps photo by Lance Cpl. Andreas A. Plaza.*

Right bottom: *Aceh, Sumatra, Indonesia (Jan. 5, 2005) – Secretary of State Colin Powell speaks to members of the international press about the United States involvement in disaster relief at a press conference held at the Banda Aceh, airport. U.S. Navy photo by Photographer's Mate 3rd Class Gabriel Piper.*

Below: *Indonesia (Jan. 14, 2005) - Life must go on... The people of Banda Aceh, Sumatra, continue to rebuild their lives following the devastating Tsunami which destroyed most of the homes in the region. U.S. Navy photo by Photographer's Mate 3rd Class Tyler J. Clements.*

THE WORLD BECOMES ONE

Right: *Island of Sumatra, Indonesia (Jan. 6, 2005) - Indonesian children smile and cheer as U.S. Navy helicopters from USS Abraham Lincoln (CVN 72) fly in purified water and relief supplies to a small village on the Island of Sumatra. U.S. Navy photo by Photographer's Mate 3rd Class Tyler J. Clements.*

Below: *Island of Sumatra, Indonesia (Jan. 13, 2005) – Indonesian citizens show their appreciation as an MH-60S Knighthawk assigned to Helicopter Combat Support Squadron Five (HC-5) departs the area, after delivering a load of humanitarian relief supplies. U.S. Navy Photo By Photographer's Mate 3rd Class Rebecca J. Moat.*

During one of their delivery missions, Sergeant Kevin Kolb said he noticed a young boy circling outside the rotor pad. Worried about his safety, Sergeant Kolb approached him. The boy's eyes lit up as the airman got closer and then he gave Sergeant Kolb a hug. When the boy left, he kissed the back of the gunner's hand to show his appreciation of their help.

There were other problems to be dealt with in Sri Lanka, as well as the immediate ones caused by the tsunami. Chinese light anti-personnel mines of type T-72A, left after the two-decade civil war, were washed up and spread by the surge of water. One of the groups called in to help, The Norwegian Peoples Organisation, assembled a team of mine sweepers to deal with the situation.

As with other tsunami-torn countries, the relief efforts in Sri Lanka carried on well into the New Year. Between January 6 and 8, 200 members of the Canadian Disaster Assistance Response Team (DART), a Canadian Forces group, arrived with four water purification units and provided medical, engineering and communication services.

As if a curse was set to blight this beautiful country forever, heavy monsoon rains fell, washing out roads and making an already gruelling situation nearly impossible for both inhabitants and those arriving to help. But humanitarian groups rose to the challenge.

Red Cross volunteers trained in disaster response, evacuated affected people and gave first aid to the injured. Representatives from Save the Children — which received a £500,000 donation from the Norwegian government for immediate relief in Sri Lanka — worked along the coast from Jaffna in the north of the island down to Galle in the south. They provided sheets, candles and washing powder to 33, 000 families. Heavy rain, as if tears from heaven, slowed down rescue efforts, but no-one gave up.

Two UN purification plants arrived on the Sumatran island of Nias within days of the disaster. World Health Organisation teams evacuated severely injured people to the mainland towns of Medan, Sibolga and Meulaboh. Shortly after, a 1,000-bed hospital ship arrived, having been dispatched from America. After initial clearing work in the northeast district of Trincomalee, World Vision partnered with a local government organisations to fund the distribution of fishing nets, small canal boats, push bikes and weighing scales. Tin sheeting for roofs, school uniforms and shoes and socks for children were also given out. It organised the establishment of general health clinics in 19 locations in tsunami-affected districts of Ampara and Batticaloa in the east and Mullaitivu and Jaffan districts in the north. It also embarked upon a cleaning project of 400 wells in areas where water had been contaminated and the construction of 216 new wells.

In the Kalutara District, the group organised hospital rehabilitation, school reconstruction, provisions of uniforms and other clothing needs, desks and chairs to 3,000 schoolchildren living in welfare camps, construction of toilets, provision of water and sanitation equipment for welfare camps and the provision of temporary housing. In the district of Galle, it helped with the clearance of debris, the rebuilding of irrigation and canal sites and started digging the foundations for temporary housing. World Vision also developed a school-feeding programme in several affected areas.

In all, the group helped around 50,000 people in Sri Lanka alone. Groups such as World Vision and CARE responded to help in tsunami-stricken India by providing cooked food to thousands of families within the first six hours. The emergency relief phase then reached out to more than 45,000 families, with food, clothes, blankets and medicines in 11 locations as well as over 1, 000 temporary shelters in Cuddalore and Nagapattinam. CARE also provided water purification tablets, oral re-hydration salts, tarpaulin sheets, plastic mats and sheets, jerry cans, blankets for temporary shelter, hygiene kits and family kits.

After its immediate response, World Vision moved into a one-year rehabilitation phase when items including educational materials and other basic household goods will be provided to 20,000 families. It was hoped that the livelihood of all those people would be "restored and stabilized" by the end of 2007.

THE WORLD BECOMES ONE

Above: *Children of Banda Aceh, Sumatra, play on the only recognisable part that remains of their home, picture taken January 14, 2005 by U.S. Navy Photographer's Mate 3rd Class Tyler J. Clements.*

One teenage girl's description of how the world answered the call to devastated Sri Lanka went around the globe. Called *The Power of Humanity*, it first appeared in *The Daily News*, Colombo, on January 19, 2005, and then on the newspaper's website. Here are extracts of the essay by 16-year-old Thrishana Pothupitiya of Sri Lanka's Bishop's College, Colombo.

"The tidal wave shattered Sri Lanka but it could not break the power of humanity. It was human kindness and compassion that reached out to the people of our land and out pouring of love, of generosity, that overwhelmed our nation... Children sold their Christmas presents in the UK to raise funds for the tsunami victims in the Asia-Pacific, the dollars, the yen, the pounds, the rupees flowed in of every currency from virtually every land.

"People are giving without a thought for themselves, as they see the devastation day in, day out, on their television screens — reality television at its worst and yet out of this disaster comes hope, hope in the form of human compassion and kindness.

"They come from all parts of the world to rebuild our land. To rebuild schools and whole communities washed away by the giant wave.

"It is the strength of humanity. Disasters bind us together with chords that cannot be broken. Chinese, Koreans, Japanese, Americans, Britons, Swedes, Australians, Germans, French, Nigerians, Arabs, Singaporeans among the multi-national, multi-coloured kaleidoscope of humanity all working together to help Sri Lanka.

"They say it will take 10 years and billions of dollars to rebuild Sri Lanka. But more than the colour of money, it is the colour of humanity. The same blood that runs through the veins of humanity has reached out to help the distressed and the dying in Sri Lanka. It was an act of love. An act of compassion. An act of humanity.

"The great Martin Luther King said: 'An individual has not started living until he can rise above the narrow confines of his individualistic concerns to the broader concerns of all humanity.'

"This disaster has been a fine example of the people of the world going beyond the narrow concerns of themselves and embracing humanity in South East Asia.

"We are surrounded by teams helping our fellow men from all four corners of the earth. This has never ever happened in Sri Lanka and we have never ever had such a disaster such as a devastating tsunami. But we can drink from the cup of human kindness, we can gain strength from that solidarity and support. Just as a child who has fallen, raises her hands to seek help to stand on her own two feet, the world has come to our aid and has extended hands of friendship, love and support.

"The ties of humanity will help us to get through this ordeal. We will one day stand up on our own two feet again, and we will rise like the proverbial phoenix. We will say thank you to human beings of all nationalities, creed and colour who came to our aid, who responded to the call of Mother Lanka in her hour of need.

"Ten years down the line there will be a new, vibrant, positive, compassionate Sri Lanka and we pray that it will be a vision of Sri Lanka at peace with herself and her fellow men.

"We will draw strength from those simple acts of humanity that helped us, extending hands of friendship and support when we fell as the water rushed at us and threatened to flow over our souls. We will never forget."

Above: *(Jan. 16, 2005) - Indonesian locals from the remote village of Lho Kruet on the island of Sumatra, Indonesia, make their way to their camp after being issued food and water distributed by the Indonesian Army while an Assessment Team from the United Nations World Health Organization survey the damage inflicted by the Tsunami. U.S. Navy photo by Photographer's Mate 3rd Class James R. McGury.*

THE WORLD BECOMES ONE

Right: *Indian Ocean (Feb. 3, 2005) - Commander Carrier Strike Group Nine (CSG-9), Rear Adm. Doug Crowder points to sailors gathered on the flight deck while holding a framed photo of an Indonesian women with a sign pleading "U.S. Soldiers Don't Leave". The picture was given to him by the U.S. Ambassador to Indonesia, the Honorable Lynn Pascoe, during a farewell ceremony thanking the crew of the Nimitz-class aircraft carrier USS Abraham Lincoln (CVN 72) and embarked Carrier Air Wing Two (CVW-2) for their involvement in Operation Unified Assistance. U.S. Navy photo by Photographer's Mate 3rd Class James R. McGury.*

Below: *Sumatra, Indonesia (Jan. 16, 2005) - Aviation Machinist's Mate 3rd Class Jason Shireman, of Chicago, Ill., gestures to another air crewman for help, as he passes out supplies to locals in a village just inland from the coast of the Island of Sumatra, Indonesia. Shireman is assigned to the "Gunbearers" of Helicopter Combat Support Squadron Eleven (HC-11), Detachment Two, of helicopters and sailors assigned to the USS Abraham Lincoln (CVN 72) Carrier Strike Group. U.S. Navy photo by Photographer's Mate 3rd Class M. Jeremie Yoder.*

It was America that spearheaded the massive undertaking to rebuild the lives and countries that the killer wave had devastated. Authorised under section 491 of the Foreign Assistance Act to "carry out and co-ordinate international disaster relief, rehabilitation and reconstruction assistance", the USA knew it had a monumental task on its hands. Within hours of the disaster, it had made contact with 50 Disaster Assistance Response Teams. In Indonesia, India, Sri Lanka and Thailand, 100 Agency for International Development (USAID) staff were already co-ordinating relief and reconstruction work.

US military efforts were awe-inspiring. Under the title 'Operation Unified Assistance', a massive humanitarian strategy was put into action. Some 20 US naval vessels and 85 US military aircraft delivered supplies to the survivors and around 15,156 US Navy, Marine, Army, Air Force and Coast Guard service members were involved in providing relief support. Millions of pounds of supplies and fresh water were delivered by helicopter and other means.

Yet, as we were to discover, this concerted act of charity and compassion did not necessarily win the recognition and praise it so richly deserved...

In the wake of the disaster, the United States formed a coalition with Australia, India and Japan to co-ordinate aid efforts to streamline immediate assistance, although, at the Jakarta Summit on January 6, the coalition transferred responsibilities to the United Nations.

The global relief projects and their funding did not always proceed in a positive way. On December 27, the very day after the Tsunami, the UN Undersecretary-General for Humanitarian Affairs, Jan Egeland, reportedly described charitable contributions from rich countries as "stingy". Speaking at a press conference later, Mr Egeland said he had been misinterpreted and stated: "It has nothing to do with any particular country or the response to this emergency. We are in early days and the response has so far been overwhelmingly positive."

By this time however, the US government, led by President George W Bush and Secretary of State Colin Powell, had reacted with annoyance to the alleged statement and added another $20 million to their original pledge of $15 million. On December 31, the US pledge was increased ten-fold to $350 million. This figure was to increase even more.

On January 5, as countries jockeyed to make large donations, Egeland said: "I'd rather see competitive compassion than no compassion." At the same time, there were complaints that pledges of money were not being honoured. Some tsunami-stricken countries also had to publicly announce that various donated goods, although dispatched in good faith, were of no use.

Sri Lanka's Foreign Minister, Laxman Kadirgamar, stated in a BBC interview: "A lot of aid which has been coming in latterly is, I'm sorry to say, not very useful. For instance, there was a container full of teddy bears. They're obviously given with good will, nobody says no to that. And we do not need rice, we are expecting a bumper harvest. Anyone who sends rice is wasting their time and money."

A spokesman for the Israeli army told the news organisations that before the extent of the disaster was clear, Sri Lanka also refused Israel's offers of aid, objecting to the inclusion of 60 Israeli soldiers in the 150-person mission to set up field hospitals, including internal medicine and paediatric clinics. The Israeli humanitarian organisation Latet sent a jumbo jet carrying 18 metric tons of supplies to Colombo, however, and a rescue-and-recovery team from the Jewish ultra-Orthodox organisation Zaka arrived with equipment used for identifying bodies, as well as body bags.

On February 1, former US President Bill Clinton was elected special UN envoy for tsunami relief. Speaking that month, he said the enormity of the task could never be underestimated. "The human price these people have paid alone argues for a commitment," said Mr Clinton, who promised to spend at least two years on the UN effort.

"This is a problem that is nowhere near solved and we can't lose our concentration on it. Now we are in a period where we're finished sending water and water pills and emergency food but the homes haven't been rebuilt, the jobs haven't all been restored, not all of the fishing boats have been replaced, the sanitation facilities have not all been reconstructed, the wells haven't all been dug. We have a moral obligation to build these areas back better than they were before the crisis began."

OPERATION UNIFIED ASSISTANCE

The scale of the US military's relief effort is best illustrated by the official report of activity in early January under the umbrella heading of 'Operation Unified Assistance'...

Helicopters assigned to Carrier Air Wing Two (CVW-2) and sailors from the USS Abraham Lincoln conducted humanitarian operations. The Abraham Lincoln Carrier Strike Group was present in the Indian Ocean off the waters of Indonesia and Thailand. The first US ship arrived from Northeast Asia on January 5 and another on January 6, with more following on. Six maritime pre-positioning ships arrived with supplies and a built-in capacity for making and pumping fresh water. The US Navy's floating hospital ship, the USS Mercy was also present.

The US military provided logistical support and responded to requests for assistance from Indonesia, Thailand and Sri Lanka. Other countries such as Japan, New Zealand, France, Germany, China, Australia, Malaysia, India, South Korea, Pakistan, Singapore and the United Kingdom contributed medical teams, field hospitals, engineers, fixed-wing aircraft and helicopters among other critical assets.

A variety of specialists were provided to US Pacific Command including crisis planners, both in Hawaii and in Thailand. Forces Command deployed four mortuary affairs teams from Fort Lee, Virginia. These teams provide tailored disaster response for mass casualty incidents worldwide and help with identification, processing, and evacuation of deceased.

The 8th US Army in Korea deployed medical and logistics units, including CH-47 Chinook helicopters. These units provided medical treatment, evacuation and supply distribution capabilities.

The US Army Corps of Engineers deployed three Forward Engineering Support Teams, from Japan, Alaska and Little Rock, Arkansas. Each FEST consisted of: One military team leader, one Civil Engineer, one Structural Engineer, one Geo-technical Engineer, and two electric power generation engineers. These teams assisted with infrastructure assessment and reconstruction planning.

The US Army Special Operations Command, Ft. Bragg, NC deployed three civil affairs teams and one Psychological Operations assessment team. The CA teams consisted of one planning team and two CA teams for co-ordinating relief efforts. The PSYOP assessment team, with its broadcast and production capabilities, focussed on information distribution in concert with local officials and relief organizations in the region.

Left: *The Operation Unified Assistance logo. The logo was approved January 15 and represents the supplies given to the affected people of Thailand, Sri Lanka and Indonesia. U.S. Marine Corps illustration by Lance Cpl. Michael J. Devoe, Jr.*

Previous page: *Indian Ocean (Jan. 1, 2005) – Seahawk helicopters assigned to Helicopter Anti-Submarine Squadron Two (HS-2) "Golden Falcons" and Helicopter Anti-Submarine Light Squadron Forty-Seven (HSL-47) "Saberhawks," depart USS Abraham Lincoln (CVN 72) en route to Aceh, Sumatra. The helicopters are transporting supplies, bringing in disaster relief teams and supporting humanitarian airlifts to tsunami-stricken coastal regions. U.S. Navy photo by Photographer's Mate 3rd Class Tyler J. Clements.*

Below: *Indian Ocean (Jan. 2, 2005) - An SH-60F Seahawk Helicopter assigned to Helicopter Anti-Submarine Squadron Two (HS-2) prepares to leave the village of Lamno, Sumatra, after inserting Indonesian Armed Forces into the village to help with humanitarian efforts. U.S. Navy photo by Photographer's Mate 2nd Class Philip A McDaniel.*

Right top: *Meulaboh, Sumatra, (Jan. 6, 2005) - Aviation Warfare Systems Operator 2nd Class Maxwell Bjerke of San Diego, Calif., surveys the damage to Meulaboh, Sumatra, during a humanitarian aid flight in an SH-60F Seahawk helicopter. U.S. Navy photo by Photographer's Mate Airman Jordon R. Beesley.*

Right bottom: *Meulaboh, Sumatra, (Jan. 7, 2005) – A Navy HH-60H Seahawk helicopter, assigned to the "Golden Falcons" of Helicopter Anti-Submarine Squadron Two (HS-2), delivers relief supplies at a mosque in the town of Meulaboh. U.S. Navy photo by Photographer's Mate 3rd Class Benjamin D. Glass.*

THE WORLD BECOMES ONE

Left: *Banda Aceh (January 6, 2005-1000)- A Naval Officer from USS Abraham Lincoln Strike Group carries an injured young boy from an MH-60S helicopter to a triage site set up by various relief groups on the Sultan Iskandar Muda Air Force Base in Band Aceh, Sumatra. U.S. Navy photo by Photographerís Mate Airman Jordon R. Beesley.*

Below: *Island of Sumatra (Jan. 7, 2005) – An SH-60B Seahawk helicopter, assigned to the "Saberhawks" of Helicopter Anti-Submarine Squadron Light Four Seven (HSL-47), lands to distribute relief supplies at a village in the island of Sumatra. U.S. Navy photo by Photographer's Mate 3rd Class Jacob J. Kirk.*

Previous page: *Island of Sumatra (Jan. 7, 2005) – An SH-60B Seahawk helicopter, assigned to the "Saberhawks" of Helicopter Anti-Submarine Squadron Light Four Seven (HSL-47), hovers over a large group of Indonesian citizens as it drops food, water and relief supplies in a Sumatran village. U.S. Navy photo by Photographer's Mate 3rd Class Jacob J. Kirk.*

Below: *Tjalang, Sumatra (Jan. 9, 2005) - Indonesian Navy landing craft and a U.S. Navy Seahawk helicopter deliver relief supplies and evacuate Indonesian citizens in Tjalang, Sumatra. U.S. Navy photo by Photographer's Mate Airman Jordon R. Beesley.*

Right top: *Meulaboh, Sumatra (Jan. 10, 2005) - Landing Craft Air Cushion (LCAC) vehicles and Marine CH-46 Sea Knight helicopters, assigned to USS Bonhomme Richard (LHD 6) and Expeditionary Strike Group Five (ESG-5), deliver much needed materials and supplies to the citizens in the city of Meulaboh, on the island of Sumatra. U.S. Navy photo by Photographer's Mate 1st Class Bart A. Bauer.*

Right bottom: *Meulaboh, Sumatra (Jan. 10, 2005) - Landing Craft Air Cushion (LCAC) vehicles, assigned to USS Bonhomme Richard (LHD 6) and Expeditionary Strike Group Five (ESG-5), deliver much needed materials and supplies to the citizens of Meulaboh. U.S. Navy photo by Photographer's Mate 1st Class Bart A. Bauer.*

Previous page: *Meulaboh, Sumatra (Jan. 10, 2005) - Landing Craft Air Cushion (LCAC) vehicles, assigned to USS Bonhomme Richard (LHD 6) and Expeditionary Strike Group Five (ESG-5), deliver materials and supplies to the citizens in the city of Meulaboh. The LCACs are capable of transporting more supplies than helicopters in a single trip. U.S. Navy photo by Photographer's Mate 1st Class Bart A. Bauer.*

Below: *Persian Gulf (Jan. 10, 2005) - An MH-53E Sea Dragon helicopter, assigned to the "Blackhawks" of Helicopter Mine Countermeasures Squadron Fifteen (HM-15), lands on the flight deck aboard the amphibious assault ship USS Essex (LHD 2). U.S. Navy photo by Photographer's Mate 3rd Class Travis M. Burns.*

Right top: *Tjalang, Sumatra (Jan. 11, 2005) – An Indonesian man gives a thumbs-up to a crew chief in the rear of an SH-60B Seahawk, assigned to the "Saberhawks" of Helicopter Anti-Submarine Squadron Light Four Seven (HSL-47), after dropping-off food and relief supplies in the village of Tjalang on the island of Sumatra. U.S. Navy photo by Photographer's Mate 3rd Class Bernardo Fulle.*

Right bottom: *Banda Aceh, Sumatra (Jan. 12, 2005) - Aerial view of one of the villages that has been set up to house Indonesians who were left homeless because of the devastating Tsunami. U.S. Navy photo by Photographer's Mate Airman Robert Kelley.*

Left top: *Andaman Sea (Jan. 12, 2005) – F/A-18E/F Super Hornets assigned to Carrier Air Wing Two (CVW-2), are prepared for launch on the flight deck aboard USS Abraham Lincoln (CVN 72). U.S. Navy photo by Photographer's Mate Airman Cristina R. Morrison.*

Left bottom: *Island of Sumatra (Jan. 12, 2005) – An MH-60S Knighthawk helicopter, assigned to the "Gunbearers" of Helicopter Combat Support Squadron Eleven (HC-11), Detachment Two, idles on a provincial road outside of Banda Aceh, as air crewmen pass out relief supplies. U.S. Navy photo by Photographer's Mate 3rd Class M. Jeremie Yoder.*

MILITARY MANPOWER SUPPORT (AS OF 11 JANUARY 2005)

- *Marines from 3rd Force Service Support Group stationed in Okinawa, Japan have landed in Sri Lanka.*
- *Marine Heavy Helicopter Squadron-362 (HMH-362) at Marine Corps Base Hawaii.*
- *100 Marines and Sailors from Marine Aviation Logistics Squadron-24 (MALS-24).*
- *6 CH-53D Sea Stallion helicopters to be airlifted by C-5 Galaxy cargo aircraft.*
- *1st Marine Aircraft Wing at Marine Corps Base Camp Butler, Okinawa, Japan: Medium and heavy lift helicopters.*
- *4 C-130s to deliver relief personnel and supplies and to conduct medical evacuations.*
- *3rd Marine Aircraft Wing at Marine Corps Air Station Miramar, California.*
- *KC-130s to Colombo, Sri Lanka to assist ESG-5.*
- *9th Communications Battalion, at Camp Pendleton, California, depart for Phuket, Thailand, to provide essential communications support throughout the area.*

TOTALS IN ACTION	*SHIPS ON STATION*
Afloat: 12,692	*25 US Navy ships*
On Ground: 2,464	*1 US Coast Guard vessel*
Thailand: 1,327	*SHIPS EN ROUTE:*
Sri Lanka: 562	*2 US Navy ships*
Indonesia: 362	
Malaysia: 213	

AIRCRAFT ON STATION	AIRCRAFT EN ROUTE
6 C-5 Heavy Lift cargo aircraft	*2 C-130 Medium Lift cargo aircraft*
4 C-17 Heavy Lift cargo aircraft	
4 C-2 Medium Lift cargo aircraft	
21 C-130 Medium Lift cargo aircraft	
6 P-3 Reconnaissance aircraft	
2 KC-135 Medium Lift/refueling aircraft	

HELICOPTERS ON STATION	HELICOPTERS EN ROUTE
51 helicopters are in the region, comprising...	*6 helicopters*
16 helicopters from USS Abraham Lincoln Carrier Strike Group	
22 helicopters from USS Bonhomme Richard Expeditionary Strike Group	
3 helicopters from USS Duluth	
10 land-based helicopters	

THE WORLD BECOMES ONE

Left top: *Island of Sumatra (Jan. 12, 2005) - An MH-60S Knighthawk helicopter, assigned to the "Gunbearers" of Helicopter Combat Support Squadron Eleven (HC-11), Detachment Two, prepares to land in a village in which little remains following the Tsunami. U.S. Navy photo by Photographer's Mate 3rd Class M. Jeremie Yoder.*

Left Bottom: *Meulaboh, Indonesia (Jan. 13, 2005) - A Landing Craft Air Cushion (LCAC) vehicle, assigned to USS Bonhomme Richard (LHD 6) and Expeditionary Strike Group Five (ESG-5), kicks up sand as it lands on the beach at Meulaboh, Indonesia. U.S. Marine Corps photo by Lance Cpl. Scott L. Eberle.*

Below: *Meulaboh, Indonesia (Jan. 13, 2005) - Sailors and Marines assigned to USS Bonhomme Richard (LHD 6) load pallets that are used to transport food and water to the victims of the tsunami on a Landing Craft Air Cushion (LCAC) assigned to Assault Craft Unit Five (ACU-5). U.S. Navy Photo by Photographer's Mate 3rd Class Jenniffer Rivera.*

THE WORLD BECOMES ONE

Left: *Meulaboh, Indonesia (Jan. 13, 2005) - A Landing Craft Air Cushion (LCAC), departs the beach landing area in route to USS Bonhomme Richard (LHD 6) after delivering disaster relief supplies. U.S. Navy photo by Chief Photographer's Mate Jerry Woller.*

Below: *Anse Boileau District, Seychelles (Jan. 13, 2005) – Sailors assigned to the guided missile cruiser USS Hue City (CG 66), volunteer their time to assist citizens of Seychelles by cleaning up the island during a scheduled port visit. U.S. Navy photo.*

Above: *Banda Aceh, Sumatra (Jan. 14, 2004) - A military support ship navigates off the coast of Banda Aceh. U.S. Navy photo by Photographer's Mate Airman Jordon R. Beesley.*

Left top: *Island of Sumatra (Jan. 13, 2005) – Local military members and victims of the Tsunami take cover from the dust and debris swept up by a departing MH-60S Knighthawk assigned to the "Providers" of Helicopter Combat Support Squadron Five (HC-5). U.S. Navy Photo By Photographer's Mate 3rd Class Rebecca J. Moat.*

Left Bottom: *Andaman Sea (Jan. 14, 2005) - An MH-60S Knighthawk helicopter, assigned to the "Gunbearers" of Helicopter Combat Support Squadron Eleven (HC-11), lowers cargo onto the deck of the Military Sealift Command (MSC) combat stores ship USNS San Jose (T-AFS 7) as the MSC fast combat support ship USNS Rainier (T-AOE 7) operates in the background. U.S. Navy photo by Photographer's Mate Airman Patrick M. Bonafede.*

Mr Clinton said his job was also to make sure governments lived up to their pledges and subsequently account for how the billions of dollars were spent. The affected nations were given six to nine months to draw up recovery plans.

Said USAID administrator Andrew Natsios in a speech in February 2005: "The response of the American people — individuals as well as civic associations, churches and corporations — has been overwhelming. Americans have donated more than $800 million to humanitarian agencies, a total second only to 9/11."

In that same month, President Bush pledged his commitment to tsunami relief. He called for $950 million "as part of the supplemental appropriations request to support the areas recovering from the tsunami and to cover the cost of relief efforts to date. This amount includes an additional $600 million above my initial commitment of $350 million."

Previous page: *Indian Ocean (Jan. 14, 2005) — An MH-60S Knighthawk helicopter, assigned to the "Gunbearers" of Helicopter Combat Support Squadron Eleven (HC-11), Detachment Two, transports cargo pallets to the dock landing ship USS Fort McHenry (LSD 43) during a vertical replenishment. U.S. Navy photo by Photographer's Mate 3rd Class M. Jeremie Yoder.*

Right: *Indian Ocean (Jan. 18, 2005) — Two helicopters assigned to Carrier Air Wing Two (CVW-2) bring supplies from the Military Sealift Command combat stores ship USNS Niagara Falls (T-AFS 3) aboard the USS Abraham Lincoln (CVN 72). U.S Navy photo by Photographer's Mate Airman Cristina R. Morrison*

Below: *Indonesia (Jan. 16, 2005) — Members of a CH-46 Helicopter crew assigned to Marine Medium Helicopter 262 (HMM-262), Futemna Marine Corps Air Station, Japan, unload humanitarian aid and disaster relief supplies in a remote region in Indonesia only accessible by helicopter. U.S. Air Force photo by Technical Sgt. Scott Reed.*

Previous page: *Banda Aceh, Sumatra (Jan. 27, 2005) - Trucks line up near a recently reconstructed bridge to cross near Banda Aceh, while the old bridge, destroyed in the Tsunami, lie in a river next to it. U.S. Navy photo by Photographer's Mate 2nd Class Seth C. Peterson.*

Left top: *Banda Aceh, Sumatra (Jan. 21, 2005) – An Aerial view near the coastline of Sumatra, shows the Indonesian people's attempt to attract aid from a passing U.S. Navy helicopter carrying relief supplies. U.S. Navy photo by Photographer's Mate 3rd Class Benjamin D. Glass.*

Left bottom: *Pearl Harbor, Hawaii (Jan. 22, 2005) - Sailors man the rails and render honors to the USS Arizona Memorial as the Nimitz-class aircraft carrier USS Ronald Reagan pulls into Naval Station Pearl Harbor. U.S. Navy photo by Photographer's Mate 1st Class James Thierry.*

Below: *Banda Aceh, Sumatra (Feb. 12, 2005) – Two U.S. Navy sailors carry an injured Indonesian man on a stretcher from an MH-60S Seahawk helicopter. U.S. Navy photo by Journalist 1st Class Joshua Smith.*

President Bush added: "We will use these resources to provide assistance and to work with the affected nations on rebuilding vital infrastructure that re-energizes economies and strengthens societies."

The money pledged was the largest amount ever in American history for a foreign natural disaster.

In all, nations throughout the world provided over $3 billion in aid for the tsunami-stricken areas. The Australian Government pledged $819.9 million (including a $760.6 million aid package for Indonesia), the German Government offered $660 million, the Japanese Government $500 million, the Canadian Government 425 million Canadian dollars and the World Bank $250 million.

The countries directly affected put their own plans of financial support together. The Malaysian government announced that MYR 1,000 ($260) would be given to families of victims while MYR 200 ($50) would be paid to those who had sustained injuries from the tsunami. Displaced residents would be given MYR 200 to alleviate their hardship, MYR 2,000 for every house damaged and MYR 5,000 for every house destroyed, while fishermen whose boats were lost will

be given MYR 1,000 for smaller boats and MYR 3,000 for larger boats.

In line with other countries, Great Britain's Disasters Emergency Committee, an umbrella group of 12 aid agencies, processed hundreds of thousands of cheques and credit card donations from the public. By the end of January 2005, these totalled £1 million, but by the time the appeal closed at midnight on February 26, the total had reached a staggering £300 million (about $550 million).

On April 6, 2005, UNICEF announced it planned to spend $90 million on rebuilding schools in Indonesian provinces devastated by the Tsunami. The money would be spent on repairing 200 schools and rebuilding 300 more. The United Nations body, which works for the welfare of children, said it also hoped to train more than 1,200 new teachers. Official sources said around 1,750 primary school teachers were dead or missing after the tragedy and more than 180,000 children had no schools to go to. "We are going to get kids back to school in a permanent way. A school is the core of the community," said spokesman John Budd.

That same month, on April 25, Bill Clinton predicted tough times ahead for the tsunami-hit regions unless donors made good their aid pledges. He said: "It's the middle period where we are now that is most difficult; where I predict you will see the largest number of newspaper stories you wish you didn't have to read, after reading how wonderful it was in the aftermath of the tragedy, when everyone was working together. It's understandable but not acceptable."

At that same time, at UN headquarters, a group of 200 US executives known as the Business Roundtable, met to combine their fund-raising efforts. President

Below: *Indian Ocean (Feb. 25, 2005) – The High Speed Vessel Two (HSV 2) Swift underway in the Indian Ocean, off the coast of Sumatra, Indonesia. U.S. Navy photo by Photographer's Mate 3rd Class Rebecca J. Moat.*

Above: *Strait of Juan De Fuca, Puget Sound, Washington (Mar. 4, 2005) – The Nimitz-class aircraft carrier USS Abraham Lincoln (CVN 72) transits the Strait of Juan De Fuca as they prepare to return to Naval Station Everett, Wash., after a deployment to the Western Pacific Ocean. U.S. Navy photo by Photographer's Mate 3rd class Chris Otsen.*

Bush joined with Bill Clinton to ask people to "reach deep into their pockets" to help those affected by the disaster.

Some pockets appeared not to be very deep, however — to the anger of villagers in India's Andaman and Nicobar Islands. In April 2005, they denounced as "paltry" compensation relief they had just received from the local government. One woman got the equivalent of five US cents for damage to her cashew nut crops. The cheque for two rupees was sent to the less than aptly named Charity Champion, who lives in the village of Nancowrie, on one of the worst hit islands. "You don't pay two rupees even for a broken window pane," she said, and pointed out that her nearest bank demands a deposit of 500 rupees to open an account. Another victim, Daniel Yunus, of Malacca in the Car Nicobar islands, received only 41

rupees (just under one US dollar) as compensation for damage to 200 areca nut trees and 300 banana trees. India's central government, which had promised millions of dollars worth of aid to the islands after the Tsunami, disputed the figures and stated that the compensation has been paid according to "objective reality".

Some months after the Tsunami, a few victim countries were asking for no more relief items to be sent. In some cases this was because affected regions already had huge stockpiles. Then the Sri Lankan government cancelled the temporary suspension of its 100 per cent tax levy on goods entering the country. All this led to controversy with 'aid mountains' failing to reach their destination.

According to a statement from Oxfam in June 2005, aid was often being distibuted disproportionately with landowners and businesses prioritised, leaving many of the poorest communities still deperately needing help.

At about the same time, a report by the group Action Aid claimed that some countries were failing to deliver the cash they had promised to stricken countries. Only Japan had provided 100 per cent of the aid it had said it would give, with Britain being the second most dependable nation, paying 97 per cent of the cash its government had pledged.

Roger Yates of Action Aid said: "Donor governments have to understand there continues to be a very real crisis in these countries. If they fail to deliver on their financial commitments, as they sometimes have with other emergencies in the past, then the work of rebuilding communities will be all that much harder".

The world might not have got it exactly right when it opened its heart after a tragedy of such epic proportions, but it did show that, in times often labelled cynical, compassion still thrives.

As with the disaster itself, there were tales of humanity and great compassion to be told from the relief and rescue missions. One of these was that involving USAID Food for Peace Officer Herbie Smith and the *USS Abraham Lincoln* which was deployed to bring fresh water to Sumatra. The *Lincoln*, offshore at Banda Aceh, could produce tens of thousands of gallons of drinkable water but there was no way to get it to those on shore. Mr Smith went out and bought

hundreds of water jugs from local markets through Indonesia and arranged with the military to get the jugs transported to the Lincoln. Military personnel then filled the jugs with clean water, and helicopters distributed it.

A group of 50 third-graders and fourth-graders at Heritage Elementary School in Chula Vista, California, recorded an original song, '*We are a Family*', written by their music teacher, Caryn Christensen. Part of the musical message was "*There'll be brighter days ahead. / And you will laugh again. / So we offer you this song / of hope, our friends.*" Proceeds from the CD went to Streetcats Foundation's One Heart For Kids initiative to benefit more than a dozen relief groups including Gospel for Asia. American Jewish World Service, UNICEF, Presbyterian Disaster Relief, Chabad of Thailand and Habitat for Humanity.

Below: *Indian Ocean (Mar. 16 2005) - The Military Sealift Command (MSC) hospital ship USNS Mercy (T-AH 19) sits off the coast of Banda Aceh, Indonesia, preparing for their return home. U.S. Navy photo by Photographer's Mate 2nd Class Jeffery Russell.*

THE WORLD BECOMES ONE

At Baan Nam Khem, a small fishing village in Thailand, French supermarket chain Carrefour paid for a new school after the old one was smashed to the ground. "We will even have a gym" said the school's director, Thavich Jitprasarn, proudly. Many other organisations offered support to the little community, too, just one of the hundreds torn apart by the tsunami. Three months after the disaster, children were seen on brand new bicycles and wearing crisp new school uniforms.

Two Canadian women, Tania Garby and Sophie Wadsworth from Jasper, Alberta, used funds from a Thai dinner event they hold locally every year to benefit victims of the tsunami in Thailand. The two travelled to the Thai province of Khao Lak, one of the areas worst hit, and 'adopted' the Parnthong family who had lost everything in the tragedy. They paid off the family's outstanding debts, gave money to improve their temporary home and brought food. Said Tania, whose time in Thailand five years earlier had given her a special affinity with its people: "Every single person had an incredible story to tell. Everybody was a victim in a big way. It was as if a bulldozer went through all the businesses and resorts. Everything was demolished."

Below: *Sasebo, Japan (Mar. 19, 2005) – The amphibious dock landing ship USS Fort McHenry (LSD 43) prepares to pull pier side in her homeport of Sasebo, Japan. U.S. Navy photo by Journalist 2nd Class James Kimber.*

CHARITIES (AND BUSINESSES) INVOLVED IN TSUNAMI RELIEF AND RESCUE

The relief effort in the wake of the Tsunami was, literally, a global act of charity, with almost every country offering practical and financial help. To give an idea of the enormity of the effort, here, from an American perspective, is a list of some of the major charities involved in both relief and rescue, and their stated roles...

Action Aid.
Helping to provide relief to the most vulnerable people affected by the devastating earthquake in Asia.

American Jewish Joint Distribution Committee.
Providing emergency food, clothing and temporary shelter as well as psychosocial support services to those most critically impacted.

American Jewish World Service.
Sending humanitarian aid to the people affected by the Tsunami.

American Refugee Committee.
Providing vital supplies and services to victims still waiting for assistance in the aftermath of this tragedy.

AmeriCares.
Immediate relief for the emergency in Southeast Asia.

Association for India's Development.
Providing relief to the very remote coastal villages that few have reached.

BAPS Care International.
Provides food kitchens to distribute hot food in affected towns in India.

Campus Crusade for Christ.
Distributing food, blankets and water in India and Sri Lanka.

CARE USA.
Providing food, clean water, clothing, bedding and medicines to tsunami disaster victims.

Catholic Relief Services.
Emergency response support.

Christian Blind Mission.
Providing help to the victims, especially the most vulnerable: people with disabilities and their families.

 CHURCH WORLD SERVICE

Church World Service.
Providing emergency supplies in affected parts of Sri Lanka and Indonesia.

Concern Worldwide.
Distributing emergency survival kits and committed to the long-term recovery.

Episcopal Relief and Development.
Working with affected communities long-term to rebuild lives in South Asia.

Healing Hands International.
Distributing medical supplies/medicines, food/water and building supplies.

Humanity First, USA.
Working in Indonesia to provide disaster relief services.

CHARITIES

India Development and Relief Fund, USA.
Providing eemergency medical services including medicines, food packets, drinking water, and clothes.

International Association for Human Values.
Establishing relief camps and sending supplies for orphaned children.

International Mission Board.
Mobilizing to reach the areas virtually untouched, even by local governments.

International Orthodox Christian Charities.
Responding to earthquake disaster in South Asia.

International Relief and Development.
Helping people rebuild their livelihoods by equipping them with tools and resources to return to self sufficiency.

International Rescue Committee.
Providing medical supplies, shelter material and water storage tanks to Indonesia.

Islamic Relief.
Providing emergency relief to the victims of the earthquake and tsunamis in Southeast Asia, Sri Lanka and India.

Lions Clubs International Foundation.
Distributing food, blankets and water and working to reconstruct homes in Sri Lanka.

Mercy USA.
Providing emergency aid to those left homeless.

Nazarene Compassionate Ministries, Inc.
Distributing Crisis Care Kits to those in need in Sri Lanka.

NetAid.
Meeting the emergency needs of thousands in areas devastated by earthquake and tsunamis.

Operation Blessing International.
Providing emergency aid and medical care to tsunami victims in Indonesia, Thailand and India.

Operation USA.
Aiding victims and sending additional relief shipments of medicines.

Salvation Army.
Providing immediate help in the form of water, food, clothing, medical supplies and temporary shelter, and counselling bereaved people.

Sewa International, USA.
Providing rescue and relief services to the victims by supplying them with food, temporary shelter, clean water, medication and survival kits.

Spiritual Awakening Mission.
Mobilizing doctors and medical teams to provide medicines, medical supplies, equipment, and medical survival kits in devastated regions.

Tamil Rehabilitation Organization.
Providing food, medical help, transport, temporary shelters to the coastal areas of the northeast of Sri Lanka.

UNHCR.
Planning a six-month, multi-million dollar emergency relief operation for tsunami victims in the Indonesian province of Aceh and in Sri Lanka.

Food And Medicine

Action Against Hunger USA.
Providing immediate material needs to displaced families.

Catholic Medical Mission Board.
Implementing sustainable healthcare programs especially for orphans, adolescents and women in the vulnerable communities.

CitiHope International.
Providing medical supplies and medicine to victims in need.

CityTeam.
Providing water purification tanks as part of immediate relief.

Dharma Vijaya Buddhist Vihara.
Providing food, fresh Water, medical Supplies as well as long term housing for the displaced.

Direct Relief International.
Sending medical material aid to earthquake victims.

Doctors of the World-USA.
Delivering medical assistance and emergency relief in Sri Lanka and Indonesia.

Feed The Children.
Distributing food, water and disaster relief supplies to help the children.

Forgotten Children.
Distributing school kits to children who lost everything in Cuddalore and helping the widows and orphans of fishermen families in Kanniyakumari.

Food for Life Global.
Providing freshly cooked meals for the tsunami victims every day.

Food for the Hungry.
Coordinating distributions of clean water and critically needed items including food, shelter and clothing.

Heart to Heart International.
Distributing water filtration systems, reverse osmosis machines, antibiotics and other critically-needed medicines in Colombo Sri Lanka.

Helen Keller International.
Providing nutritional supplements to children, assessing living conditions and directing clean water, shelter, food, sanitation and medical care to those in need.

India Partners.
Providing medical care and orchestrating village reconstruction in seaside villages in India.

International Medical Corps.
International Medical Corps (IMC) is on the ground in Aceh, Indonesia, providing direct emergency assistance to victims of the South Asia tsunami.

International Medical Health Organization.
Providing medical care at the ground level for the victims of tsunami.

International Relief Teams.
Deploying nurses and physicians to direct distribution of medicines and set up a field hospital.

Islamic Circle of North America.
Providing food, medicine, clothes, tents & other urgently needed supplies.

Kiwanis International.
Distributing medicine and other urgently needed supplies.

Knightsbridge International.
Distributing lifesaving medicines and supplies to victims in India, Sri Lanka and Sumatra.

CHARITIES

MAP International.
Preparing shipments of medicines and medical supplies.

Mercy Airlift.
Acquiring and transporting emergency relief supplies to the victims of natural or man made disasters.

Medical Ambassadors International.
Providing direct relief to affected areas in the Tsunami impacted regions.

Mission India.
Distributing survival kits and vaccinations.

Northwest Medical Teams.
Treating the sick and wounded in Sri Lanka and Indonesia.

Oxfam.
Sending food, water and supplies to aid victims.

Project Concern International.
Working to secure a continuous supply of safe drinking water, provide medical assistance to the injured and sick.

Project Hope.
Providing medicine and medical supplies to those most in need.

Relief International.
Providing medical care to victims in Sri Lanka and committed to both short-term and long-term relief.

Rescue Corps.
Funds will be used to purchase urgently needed supplies.

Sarvodaya USA.
Sending food and medicine to coastal areas of Sri Lanka in a state of devastation.

United Nations World Food Programme.
Shipping tons of food – rice, noodles and biscuits – and liters of water into the remote regions.

World Concern.
Distributing emergency supplies to those most in need in Thailand and Sri Lanka.

CHILDREN AND FAMILIES

Baptist Child & Family Services.
Training individuals on how to run foster care systems and to train and ensure the future of the children in Sri Lanka.

Child Health Foundation.
Providing therapy to prevent dehydration and death from disease.

Children's Emergency Relief International.
Providing long-term foster care and permanent placement to the orphans of the Tsunami.

Christian Children's Fund.
Providing emergency relief to children and families.

Episcopal Relief and Development.
Working in India, Sri Lanka, Indonesia, and Thailand to provide critical assistance to vulnerable children and families.

Isaac Foundation.
Providing care to the youngest of victims in southern Thailand.

MADRE.
Providing assistance and counselling to displaced women and families.

MercyCorps.
Assisting families affected by the earthquake.

Samaritan's Purse.
Distributing clean water, emergency food, cooking supplies, temporary shelter, and medicine.

Save the Children.
Assisting children and families impacted by one of the world's most devastating earthquakes.

UNICEF.

Delivering survival supplies to coastal areas.

World Vision.

Food and Family Survival Kits to affected Asians.

REBUILD AND RECOVER

ADRA International.

Responding to and assessing the damage in Thailand, Sri Lanka, Indonesia, and India.

All India Movement for Seva.

Rehabilitating the victims in Pondicherry, Nagapatnam district and other coastal areas of India.

American Friends Service Committee.

Providing support for earthquake and tsunami survivors in Asia.

Ananda Marga Universal Relief Team (AMURT).

Planning reconstruction programs in India and Indoensia.

Architecture for Humanity.

Helping to rebuild in the earthquake's aftermath.

Asha for Education.

Assessing the impact of the disaster on projects and helping with relief and rehabilitation efforts.

Bharat Sevashram Sangha.

Rehabilitating the victims of the Tsunami.

Co-operative Housing Foundation International.

Providing shelters for displaced persons.

Correll Missionary Ministries.

Helping with clean up, search for survivors, and providing homes for the homeless.

Habitat for Humanity International.

Helping families in need of shelter in Indonesia, Sri Lanka, India, Thailand, Malaysia and Bangladesh.

The Ilankai Thamil Sangam, USA.

Providing rehabilitation and orphanage assistance to victims in the Northern and Eastern districts of Sri Lanka.

International Aid.

Evaluating the initial relief effort and co-ordinating the follow-up programs necessary to sustain the relief effort.

International Development Law Institute.

Assessing the legal dimensions of the problems which the victims will be facing in immediate term and in reconstruction.

Lutheran World Relief.

Providing relief aid with partners in India.

Mission to the World.

Setting up refugee camps and focusing on construction and counselling in Sri Lanka.

Needful Provision.

Using self-help technologies, such as solar-powered cooking ovens and solar-powered refrigerators to help victims.

Plan USA.

Orchestrating long-term reconstruction programs.

Serving Our World

Working in Thailand to help ensure that lives and families are restored.

Society of St. Vincent de Paul

Working to help re-establish families and to protect those who have lost everything.

Solar Electric Light Fund

Installing solar electric power systems for water pumping and hospitals.

Sri Lanka Foundation
Concentrating on long term relief efforts such as rebuilding houses and schools.

Surfing The Nations Foundation
Providing effective and personal relief to tsunami survivors that will allow them to sustain themselves.

United Nations Foundation
Co-ordinating aid to Tsunami survivors.

United Way International
Focusing on long-term recovery efforts.

World Missionary Evangelism.
Rebuilding homes, boats and distributing new fishing supplies so that those who lost their means of income can once again begin to provide for their families.

World Relief
Rebuilding communities in India, Sri Lanka and Indonesia

AIDING ANIMAL VICTIMS

Animal Aid

Animal People

Best Friends Animal Society

Humane Society

Noah's Wish

World Society for the Protection of Animals

BIG BUSINESS MAKES A DONATION

These are some of the major companies that made massive donations to th Tsunami relief efforts...

Pfizer
$35m ($10m cash; $ 25m medicines)

Coca-Cola
$10m

Bristol-Myers Squibb
$5m ($1m cash; $4m medicines)

ExxonMobil
Taking on the world's toughest energy challenges.

Exxon Mobil
$5m

Abbott Laboratories
$4m ($2m cash; $2 medicine))

Microsoft
$3.5m

BP
$3m

citigroup

Citigroup
$3m

JP Morgan Chase
$3m

Royal Dutch/Shell Group
$3m

UBS AG
$3m

Cisco Systems
$2.5m

AIG/The Starr Foundation
$2.5m

Wal-Mart Stores
$2m

Daimler Chrysler
$2m

Johnson & Johnson
$2m + medicines

Vodafone
GBP 1m ($1.95m)

Tetra Laval Group
$1.5m (including provision of liquid foods)

Deutsche Telekom
EUR 1m ($1.4m)

Deutsche Bank
EUR 10m ($13m)

Siemens AG
EUR 1m

Allianz Group
EUR 1m

ASF
EUR 1m

AXA Group
EUR 1m

ChevronTexaco
$1.24m

Infosys
INR 50m ($1.1m)

Altana
EUR 750,000 ($1m)

Boeing
$1m

ConocoPhillips
$1m

IBM
$1m

Nike
$1m

Pepsi
$1m + soft drinks + water

Merrill Lynch
$1m

American Express
$1m

General Electric
$1m

First Data Corp. (Parent company of Western Union Money Transfer)
$1m

General Motors
$ 1m

HSBC
$1m

Verizon Communications
$1m

ING
$1m

Qantas
AUD 1m + flights

Cable & Wireless
$1m

Dhiraagu (The Maldives' national telecommunications company)
$1m

Bayer
EUR 500,000 ($700,000)

Nestlé
CHF640,000 ($560,000)

The Home Depot
$500,000 [192]

Texas Instruments
$500,000

Carrefour
EUR 300,000 ($420,000)

Hitachi
JPY 20m ($200,000)

Hewitt Associates
$200,000

Independent News & Media
EUR 100,000

MTR Corporation Limited
HKD 0.5 per passenger trip on January 2, 2005 Projected goal: HKD 1m (roughly $128,000)

MAC
$10,000

KCR Corporation
All fares collected during the 4-hour extension service on January 1, 2005, morning.

Fonterra
Milk powder and infant formula throughout the region

Wing On Travel
Tour guides set off to affected areas to offer assistance and translation services.

National Hockey League
$100,000+.

Right: *(L-R) Tennis players Vera Zvonareva, Elena Dementieva and Maria Sharapova of Russia and Serena and Venus Williams of the U.S. pose after selling their rackets during an auction in Hong Kong to raise funds for Asian Tsunami survivors on January 8, 2005. Eight tennis players raised a total of HK$1.6 million ($205,000).*

Below: *Teams headed by football stars Shevchenko and Ronaldinho team before the match labelled "Tsunami: soccer is helping" at Nou Camp stadium in Barcelona, Spain, February 15, 2005. This match to raise funds for those affected by the Tsunami, was organised jointly by UEFA and FIFA and by mutual accord with the Spanish Football Federation and in collaboration with FC Barcelona.*

Previous page: *Fireworks light up the Sydney Harbour, Australia during New Year's Eve celebrations January 1, 2005. The celebrations, which were watched by around one million people on the foreshore and in boats, included a fund-raising appeal.*

Right: *Los Angeles Lakers' Kobe Bryant (L) drives past Houston Rockets' Tracy McGrady during the fourth quarter of the Lakers 111-104 win in Los Angeles, January 7, 2005. Bryant and McGrady were the high scorers with 27 and 26 points respectively, in a game in which they pledged to donate $1,000 for every point they scored to help victims of the Indian Ocean tsunami.*

Below: *Special Envoy to the Prime Minister of Malaysia Razali Ismail (R), Michelle Yeoh (2nd R) and members from Backstreet Boys, Boyz II Men and the Black Eyed Peas attend the Force of Nature Aid Foundation news conference in Kuala Lumpur on March 17, 2005. The Force of Nature Concert for Tsunami Aid was the first initiative of the Force of Nature Aid Foundation and was held at the Stadium Putra in Kuala Lumpur, Malaysia.*

Below: *England and Real Madrid midfielder David Beckham visits UNICEFís central supply warehouse in Copenhagen. Beckham, a newly-appointed UNICEF Goodwill Ambassador paid the visit to the warehouse on January 10, 2005 in support of the global relief effort for families affected by the Tsunami.*

Right top: *The Asian XI team poses for a shot before the World Cricket Tsunami Appeal One Day International between The Rest of the World XI and The Asian XI at the Melbourne Cricket Ground, Australia, January 10, 2005.*

Right bottom: *United Nations Secretary General Kofi Annan visits a camp for tsuanmi survivors, set up at Cabeer Jumma mosque in Hambantota, eastern Sri Lanka January 8, 2005.*

Left top: *Indonesian navy officials load logistic supplies, that will be sent to Aceh province, onto a Singapore Hercules plane at Jakarta's military base on December 30, 2004, millions of people around the Indian Ocean were scrambling for food and clean water, with the threat of disease and hunger stalking survivors of the Tsunami.*

Above: *Two elephants, Medang (R) and Ida (L), clear the debris of houses damaged by the Tsunami to make a path for vehicles in Indonesia's city of Banda Aceh, January 3, 2005.*

Left bottom: *Tsunami survivors rush for clothes and food donated by volunteer organisations in Cuddalore, about 180 km (112 miles) south of the Indian city of Madras on December 29, 2004.*

Next page: *Britain's Princes William (L) and Harry (R) help to pack items bound for victims of the Tsunami in the Maldives, at a Red Cross depot near Bristol, western England, January 7, 2005.*

Nation By Nation, The Rush To Give

Australia

Financial: An initial AUD 10 million pledge ($US 7.7 million) with two additional disbursements of AUD 25 million ($18.1 million). (AUD 10 million to aid organizations, AUD 10 million to Indonesia, and AUD 5 million ($3.6 million) to Sri Lanka. Foreign Affairs Minister Alexander Downer indicated Australia would offer further aid as needed. On January 5 2005 in Jarkarta, Prime Minister John Howard announced an Australian aid package of AUD 1 billion — significantly exceeding the half billion expected. On January 11, AUD 500,000 aid was announced for the Seychelles, taking total federal government monetary assistance to AUD 1,060,500,000. The state governments of the Australian Capital Territory, New South Wales, the Northern Territory, Queensland, South Australia, Victoria and Western Australia all pledged monetary assistance to a combined total of AUD 17.45 million ($13.6 million).

Practical: The Australian Defence Force (ADF) worked in the region, alongside American forces. Over 900 unarmed personnel in Indonesia, including 15 air-traffic controllers, managed the massive aid effort in Aceh. Eight Royal Australian Air Force C-130 Hercules assisted in the massive clean-up in Indonesia. Four Hercules moved stores within Indonesia, while another four planes established an air bridge to move material and personnel from Australia. At the outbreak of the disaster, three were immediately dispatched with essentials such as medical supplies, water purification units, blankets and bottled water. A Royal Australian Navy amphibious transport ship, HMAS Kanimbla, was dispatched from Sydney on New Year's Eve, to arrive in Indonesia on January 13, with two H-3 Sea King helicopters on board. Four Australian Army UH-1 Iroquois helicopters in Aceh, where the ADF has established a field hospital and water plant. The Australian Federal Police (AFP) also had teams on the ground, particularly in Thailand, including body identification teams. Teams of medical and emergency professionals and volunteers were despatched. In response to a request from the Maldivian Government, Australia sent ecological experts to repair coral reefs — the life-blood of Maldivian tourism — and teachers to restore schooling. The estimated cost of this additional support was above AUD 60 million ($46.5m), and was managed by Emergency Management Australia (EMA).

Acts of charity: Australia's three major commercial television networks, Seven, Nine and Ten, pooled resources to organise a special concert telethon aired on January 8, 2005. It was simultaneously broadcast on all three networks and in most capitals on the Triple M radio network. The final amount pledged was AUD 20 million. The Australian public raised over AUD 190 million ($143.37 million). As a sign of respect to the victims of the disaster, New Years Eve celebrations around the country were either toned-down or cancelled. Most celebrations that did take place included collections of money for the victims. Most of those celebrations that did proceed, organised collections for charities. Australia's largest New Year's celebration, in Sydney, alone raised over AUD 1.1 million for Oxfam-Community Aid Abroad.

Austria

Financial: The government promised EUR 50m ($65.30m).

Acts of charity: The Austrian public donated around EUR 18m.

Belgium

Financial: Belgian government sent EUR 12m ($16.4m).

Practical: Various organisations such as Artsen zonder Grenzen sent medical teams.

Acts of Charity: During a charity show on January 14, public and private media in Belgium collected more than EUR 38m.

Brazil

Practical: Initial emergency aid of 10 tonnes of food and 8 tonnes of medicine were delivered to Thailand and India by the Brazilian Air Force.

Acts of Charity: Private citizens and small businesses organised a national effort to collect food, medicine and clothes. In Rio de Janeiro, 70 tonnes donated in the city alone by locals, were delivered on January 2 to the Consul of Sri Lanka. Many more tonnes were handed to the local embassies and consulates of the countries affected.

Bulgaria

Financial: The Bulgarian Military Academy of Medicine allocated BGN 200,000 (EUR 100,000) worth of aid to Indonesia and Sri Lanka in the form of medicines and emergency equipment.

Practical: The Bulgarian Red Cross and the national emergency agency sent emergency equipment, drugs and shelters.

Cambodia

Financial: The Royal Cambodian Government donated $40,000 total: $10,000 each to India, Indonesia, Sri Lanka and Thailand.

Canada

Financial: The Canadian government pledged CAD 425m ($344.96m). It also said it would match private donations received by January 11, 2005 — this represented an additional CAD 200M. The Canadian government also announced a debt moratorium for the countries most severely effected by the Tsunami. In addition to the federal funds, the provincial government of British Columbia gave CAD 8m ($6.6m) to the Canadian Red Cross. The provincial governments of Ontario and Alberta each pledged CAD 5m ($4.1m). The provincial governments of Quebec, Manitoba, New Brunswick, Newfoundland and Labrador, and Nova Scotia each gave CAD 100,000 ($82,000), and the provincial governments of the Northwest Territories and Prince Edward Island pledged CAD 25,000 and 20,000 respectively.

Practical: Sent its DART (Disaster Assistance Response Team) to Ampara in Sri Lanka. Provided blankets, water purification devices, and generators through the Canadian International Development Agency (CIDA).

Acts of Charity: The government estimated that donations to Tsunami victims reached more than CAD 230M, with 200M of this available for matching. The federal government announced it would match donations dollar-for-dollar and decided to bend the rules by allowing Tsunami-related donations made before 11 January, 2005, to be claimed on 2004 income-tax returns.

Chile

Practical: The Chilean government sent a group of four doctors, one engineer and one architect to Indonesia. It opened a special bank account for public donations.

China

Financial: PRC government sent RMB 521.63 million ($63 million) to South and Southeast Asia. Overall donations from the Chinese public over 150 million RMB.

Hong Kong   (SAR China)

Financial: As of 7 January 2005, citizens of Hong Kong donated a total of HKD 560 million ($71.8 million).

Practical: Various NGOs, companies and individuals went to affected countries to offer assistance. The government of Hong Kong sent 120 personnel to help

Hong Kong residents and search for missing people. Police and medical teams were on stand-by to offer assistance.

Acts of charity: Performer Karen Joy Morris (aka Karen Man Wai Mok) pledged to donate HKD 200 thousand (Ming Pao). Performers of EEG also pledged to donate a total sum of HKD 630 thousand. Sir Run Run Shaw donated HKD 10m. Hong Kong Jockey Club donated HKD 10m and said it would donate HKD1 for each dollar it received from donors (target at a minimum HKD 10m). MTR donated HKD 0.5 for each passenger trip on January 2, 2005, with a total sum at HKD1m. KCR donated all the fares collected in the four-hour extension of train services on January 1 2005. Hong Kong Red Cross collected HKD 100 m (global target $46 m (HKD 360 m). World Vision Hong Kong collected HKD 50 m. A TV variety show on TVB and RTHK on January 2, 2005, collected HKD 40 m (HKET). Hutchison Whampoa Limited and Li Ka Shing Foundation of Hong Kong announced on December 28, 2004, that they would donate HKD 24 million ($3.08 million) for the relief fund.

MACAU (SAR China)
Financial: Macau Red Cross collected MOP 35 m.

CROATIA
Financial: The Croatian government allocated HRK 4m (EUR 520,000) for aid to be split equally between India, Sri Lanka, Indonesia and Thailand. Croatian Red Cross to contribute HRK 4.8m (EUR 630,000) from public donations.

CZECH REPUBLIC
Financial: The Czech government pledged CZK 200m (EUR 6.5m or $8.7m) worth of aid.
Acts of Charity: Public donations amounted to more than CZK 230m, (about $10m. The total made the country a leading donor from the former Eastern bloc.

DENMARK
Financial: The Danish government pledged aid worth DKR 300 m (EUR 40.38m). Danish Prime Minister Anders Fogh Rasmussen said that Denmark would increase this amount if deemed necessary by the UN or emergency relief organisations.

FINLAND
Financial: The Finnish government gave EUR 4.5m to help the victims of the Tsunami and a further EUR 5.5m to be given to helping aid organisations when requested. In addition, EUR 75,000 and a field hospital from the Finnish Red Cross and EUR 25,000 from Save the Children Finland sent.

FRANCE
Financial: Pledged EUR 22.16m with EUR 15m allocated to the UN's agencies and Red Cross, and EUR 1.56m used immediate assistance. Another EUR 5.6m part of this sum was the first French participation to the European aid. Some EUR 20m pledged for clean water installations.
Practical: Dispatched plane with 100 rescue personnel and 800kg of medical supplies.

GERMANY
Financial: The German government initially allocated EUR 20m ($26m) for immediate aid. Additionally, the German government will give EUR 500m over a period of three to five years for long-term-help.
Practical: Fast-response teams of the governmental technical relief organisation (THW) were sent to Thailand and Sri Lanka for rescue purposes, together with drinking water purification equipment to be installed in Galle (Sri Lanka). Additional water

purification equipment was sent to the Maledives and Indonesia on first days of 2005. Medical and supporting units of the German armed forces sent, including a supporting frigate and medevac airlifts. Australian and German forces joined to build a large-scale field hospital. The German Chancellor proposed to release the most affected countries from their debts and to create a scheme under which every EU nation 'adopts' one of the most severely affected countries and ensures long-lasting aid.

Acts of Charity: German charities, TV shows and private donations totalled more than $400m.

GREECE

Financial: Allocated EUR 0.3m ($0.4m) to the Maldives and Sri Lanka, followed by an additional EUR 1m ($1.3m).

Practical: Two planes carried 6 tonnes of humanitarian materials.

Acts of Charity: The Greek people raised over EUR 15m ($19.9m) through private donations made during a TV charity marathon which included the auction of articles such as commemorative items from the Athens Olympic Games and the Euro 2004 event, as well as the fountain pen of the retreating President of the Hellenic Republic.

HUNGARY

Practical: Hungary sent a medical and rescue team of 10 as well as two containers and ten pallets of emergency goods to Thailand and Srí Lanka.

ICELAND

Financial: The Icelandic government pledged ISK 5m ($70,000) to the Icelandic Red Cross to ensure "the money gets into the right hands". Early in 2005, the government announced the total contribution would be ISK 150m ($2.5m).

Practical: An aeroplane from Loftleixir Icelandic (a subsidiary of Flugleixir) flew to Phuket island to pick up Swedish survivors. A little under 10 tonnes of Iceland Spring Water manufactured by Ölgerxin Egill S

INDIA

Financial. The federal government pledged INR 1 billion ($23 million) to Sri Lanka and Maldives. A federal budgetary allocation of INR 7 billion ($160 million) was earmarked for immediate distribution to affected Indian provinces.

Practical: Warships and aircraft distributed relief supplies. The Japanese government provided $500 million in aid to affected countries. Emergency medical teams were sent to Indonesia, Sri Lanka, Thailand and the Maldives.

IRELAND

Financial: The Irish government pledged EUR 20m ($26.12m) Most of this was given to Irish Aid organisations and the UN.

Acts of Charity: In the immediate aftermath of the disaster, the Irish public quickly started collecting money, on the streets, in churches, schools, in shopping centres and many other initiatives such as the Work a Day for Free, where many workers throughout the country donated a days wages to the disaster relief fund. An estimated EUR 1m was raised also by pubs and hotels in collections. Hundreds of other events took place throughout the country. The various Irish charities raised over EUR 75m from the public in response to the disaster, with the Irish Red Cross, Concern, and Goal all raising several million each. The church based charity Trócaire alone raised EUR 27m over just one weekend

IRAN

Practical: Iran sent 221 tonnes of relief supplies consisting of medicine, tents, blankets, clothes and foodstuff to Indonesia as well as donating $675,000 through the Red Crescent.

ISRAEL

Practical: The Israeli government sent supplies worth $100,000 to each affected country. In addition, an Israeli medical team was dispatched to Sri Lanka, and 150 IDF doctors and rescue and relief teams were mobilised for the region with 82 tonnes of aid including 9 tonnes of medicine, nearly 4,000 litres of mineral water, 12 tonnes of food, over 17 tonnes of baby food, 10,000 blankets, tents, sheeting, as well as power generators. An additional offer of assistance to India in the form of search and rescue teams from their Home Front Command as well as food and medicine was extended and the Israeli Ministry of Health was dispatched to Thailand on a medical mission. Ultra-Orthodox Jewish forensic workers, famous in Israel for post-terror bombing victim identification for families and proper burial, were dispatched to collect and identify victims.

ITALY

Financial: The CEI (Italian Conference of Bishops) sent 100,000 euros (part of a donation of $1.7m from Caritas Internationalis) and collected national donations. The government pledged EUR 3m ($3.9m).
Practical: Five Italian flights were sent to Sri Lanka carrying an advanced team of eight experts of the Italian Civil Protection Department with 50 tonnes of equipment and goods — including two field hospitals, 20 doctors and medical staff, medical kits, field kitchens, water pumps, water storages.

Acts of Charity: Private money-raising efforts co-ordinated by newspapers and telephony companies have collected more than EUR 12.6m). The Pope authorised the immediate release of $6m to be delivered to the International Red Cross, for use in the humanitarian relief effort.

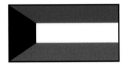

JAPAN

Financial: World's second largest donor of Official Development Assistance (known as ODA).
Practical: Dispatched Japan Self-Defense Forces vessels off Northern Sumatra to supply aid. Land, Air, and Maritime Forces were on standby.

KUWAIT

Financial: The Kuwaiti government donated KWD 3m ($10m) as humanitarian aid.

LUXEMBOURG

Financial: Donated at least EUR 5m ($6.5 million) as humanitarian aid.

MALAYSIA

Practical: Malaysia sent rescue teams abroad as its own damage was minimal. This freed the Special Malaysian Rescue Team (SMART) to fly to Indonesia. The 73-member combination unit from SMART, Malaysian Red Crescent Society Fire and Rescue Department were sent to Medan, Sumatra, with food supplies, medicine and clothing for about 2,000 victims. Additional military doctors team in a CN 235 aircraft and a Nuri helicopter sent to Aceh. Further aid was sent on C-130 Hercules transport aircraft. MERCY (Malaysian Medical Relief Society) flew to Sri Lanka. Two teams based in Kesdam Military Hospital, one of the two surviving hospitals in Banda Aceh. Malaysia opened its airspace and two airports, Subang Airport and Langkawi International Airport to relief operations and acts as a staging base to forward relief supplies to Aceh.

Mexico

Financial: The Mexican federal government pledged an aid package of $1,100,000 (MXN 12,000,000).
Practical: Search teams, known as Topos and experiences in earthquake rescue operations, were dispatched by the Ministry of Foreign Affairs (SRE). The Mexican armed forces sent a hospital ship, other vessels, and helicopters. The Mexican Red Cross also invited Mexican citizens to give aid to be distributed amongst local agencies.

Morocco

Practical: The Moroccan Foreign Ministry dispatched aid, consisting of medical supply, vaccines and blankets to Indonesia, Sri Lanka, India, Thailand, Malaysia, and the Maldives.

Mozambique

Financial: The Mozambique government gave a 'symbolic' $100,000 to an aid appeal, and encouraged businesses and individuals to donate to accounts set up by the local Red Cross.

Netherlands

Financial: The Dutch government reserved EUR 227m ($295m) for aid to the affected area.

Practical: A KDC-10 aircraft of the Dutch Airforce flew several missions to the affected areas, providing emergency supplies and a mobile hospital unit. Military air-traffic-controllers sent to Banda Aceh to help with the stream of relief flights. Also, a specialized forensic identification team helped to find the identities of dozens of Tsunami victims in Thailand.
Acts of Charity: The Dutch Red Cross dedicated EUR 100,000 ($0.13 million) for emergency aid. Several private initiatives varying from calls to give money to Samenwerkende Hulporganisaties (Giro 555) to collecting food and other supplies for the affected areas. These initiatives raised over EUR 160.5m ($208.6m).

New Zealand

Financial: Government initially announced a donation of NZD 10 million ($7.2 million). Increased this to NZD 68 million ($47.2m). The government's response included $NZ20 million ($A18.4 million) for United Nations relief efforts, $NZ20 million ($A18.4 million) for work in Aceh and other parts of Sumatra through a bilateral aid program in Indonesia and a $NZ19 million ($A17.5 million) dollar-for-dollar matching of public donations by New Zealanders.
Practical: An airfares (RNZAF) C-130 Hercules, working in unison with the Royal Australian Air Force, sent for evacuation and transport of relief supplies. New Zealand also sent an RNZAF 757 aircraft to the Thai city of Phuket with a specialist victim identification team on board.
Acts of Charity: The New Zealand government announced that it would match, dollar for dollar, the amount pledged by its citizens to various charities. By January 18, 2005, this amounted to further NZD 19million.

North Korea

Financial: The government pledged $150,000.

NORWAY

Financial: The Norwegian government allocated NOK 1.1bn ($180m) to be distributed to the UN, the Red Cross and other aid organisations. The prime minister also pledged to provide more funds as needed in aid relief co-ordinated by the United Nations. An ongoing appeal was launched to convince the government to provide a total amount of NOK 10 billion ($1.64bn) from the Norwegian Petroleum Fund.

Practical: The Royal Norwegian Air Force and Scandinavian Airlines established airlift shuttles providing emergency transport services between Thailand and Scandinavia for as long as necessary.

OMAN

Practical: Oman sent relief goods worth $3m for victims in Sri Lanka, Maldives and Indonesia.

PAKISTAN

Financial: Government announced a PKR 10 million ($0.2 million) relief package of goods such as tents, medicines, drinking water and food items for the earthquake victims of Sri Lanka.

Practical: Military Pakistan sent 500 military personnel in medical and engineering teams and two C-130 aeroplanes with relief goods and 250 doctors and engineers to Indonesia and Sri Lanka. Six more C-130s were dispatched to Indonesia and two Seaking helicopters onboard PNS (Pakistan Navy Ship) *Moawin* in Sri Lanka to provide logistics support. Navy ships Ships Khyber and Mua'awan were sent to Sri Lanka. On board were three helicopters, a marine Expeditionary Force, doctors and paramedics. Relief goods — medicines, medical equipment, food supplies, tents, blankets — were sent in huge quantities. Pakistan Navy ships, Tariq and Nasr, on a goodwill visit to the Maldives, saved 367 foreign tourists (representing 17 nationalities) conducted aerial surveys to judge the extent of damage,

distributed food and medicines, and provided medical assistance. Pakistan Navy Task Force arrived at Colombo port to provide humanitarian assistance and relief goods to the government of Sri Lanka.

POLAND

Financial: The Polish government donated PLN 1m ($0.3m) to Polish aid non-governmental organisations.

PORTUGAL

Financial: Government approved EUR 8m ($10,9m) in aid.

Practical: Sent planes with relief supplies to Sri Lanka and Indonesia.

QATAR

Financial: Qatar offered $25m, plus food, medical and logistical supplies.

ROMANIA

The Romanian government approved EUR 150,000 worth of medical aid, tents and beds to South Asia.

Acts of Charity: EUR 395,000 was raised by the public in a telethon, bringing the collected total to EUR 545,500.

RUSSIA

Practical: Two transport planes of the Russian Ministry for Emergency Situations sent to Sri Lanka carrying 110 tents and 2200 blankets with a total weight of 25 tonnes. Russia also sent a rescue helicopter Bo-105 to fly over the area to search for and evacuate people. Another plane was sent with tents, drinking water, water cleaning stations and other humanitarian aid. Field hospital equipment sent to Indonesia. Nearly 150 tons of humanitarian aid was flown to Sri Lanka, Thailand and Indonesia from December 27 to January 10. The humanitarian cargoes, part of them supplied by Belarus, included tents, blankets, bedding, water purification installations and flour.

Acts of Charity: The town of Beslan, scene of the 2004 school hostage crisis, donated RUB 1m ($36,000) from the fund set up after the hostage incident.

SAUDI ARABIA

Financial: Saudi Arabia pledged a $30m aid package, consisting of $5m worth of food, tents and medicine, to be transported and distributed via the Saudi Red Crescent, and another $5 million in funds for international aid groups such as the Red Cross and the UN High Commissioner for Refugees.

SERBIA

Financial: The Serbian government approved immediate delivery of 40 tonnes of humanitarian aid worth EUR 150,000. Two Aviogenex airplanes were provided for the delivery.

Practical: The Exit Music Festival collected 317,000 litres of water from sponsors. Serbian Red Cross collected money.

SINGAPORE

Financial: The government pledged SGD 5m to relief efforts initially, including SGD 1m in cash to the Singapore Red Cross Society (SRCS) which collected more than SGD 27m. At the emergency disaster summit in Jakarta, the government pledged an additional $10m to help victims. A government-linked investment company, Temasek Holdings, earmarked $10m for relief work.

Practical: The government offered the use of its

air and naval bases as a staging area to the United Nations and other relief agencies as well as to other countries, including the US, Australia, France and Japan. The United Nations accepted Singapore's offer to set up a UN Regional Co-ordination Centre to co-ordinate relief efforts to stricken areas The Singaporean humanitarian relief operation involved more than 1200 military and civil defence personnel — of whom 900 were directed to in Aceh, Indonesia. The humanitarian assistance provided by its military, medical and rescue teams was estimated to cost SGD 20m. Singapore has also offered to rebuild hospitals and clinics in Aceh. The Singapore Armed Forces (SAF) deployed three amphibious transport dock — *RSS Endurance*, *RSS Persistence* and *RSS Endeavour* — off the coast of Meulaboh, one of the worst hit areas where all road access was cut off. These ships carried medical and engineering teams and volunteers with NGOs. The ships were also loaded with medical supplies and heavy equipment. Singapore also dispatched six Chinook helicopters and two Super Puma helicopters to Aceh, two Chinook helicopters and two Super Puma helicopters to Phuket, Thailand. C130s were dispatched to ferry relief supplies.

SLOVENIA

Financial: The Slovenian government approved SIT 44m (EUR 185,500) for immediate delivery.

SOUTH AFRICA

Financial: The South African government's official financial contribution consisted of co-ordinated aid to the Maldives. This included sending a freighter with South African helicopters and crew, as well as emergency supplies. The Maldives was selected because, according to the South African government: "It was impossible to confirm the full extent of the damage as hardly any emergency rescue effort had taken place."

Acts of Charity: South Africans donated $2.6 million in cash and more than 280 tons of food to Tsunami relief efforts via the Red Cross.

SOUTH KOREA

Financial: The South Korean Government pledged an initial $600,000 and then an additional $1.4m.
Practical: A 20-person emergency aid team of 5 medical specialists, nurses and administrative staff was dispatched to Sri Lanka by The Korean Ministry of Health and Welfare and a medical aid group. A shipment with medicine and medical supplies worth SKW 200m ($192,000) followed.

SPAIN

Financial: The Spanish Cabinet approved an aid package totalling EUR 54m ($70.5m): EUR 4m ($5.2m) for immediate delivery, allocated to the relief shipments conducted by the Spanish Agency of International Co-operation (AECI) and NGOs; and EUR 50m Development Aid Fund (FAD) loan, with favourable terms that include long periods of repayment and low interest, aimed to support the reconstruction efforts in all countries affected by the quake. Several Governments of the Autonomous communities approved their particular aid packages for urgent delivery: Galicia (EUR 500,000), Madrid (EUR 300,000), Basque Country, (EUR 150,000), Andalucia (EUR 150,000), Valencian Community (EUR 150,000), Balearic Islands (EUR 150,000), Castilla-La Mancha (EUR 140,000), Catalonia (EUR 130,000) and La Rioja (EUR 66,000). The donations of regional governments and local councils amounted to EUR 2m.
Practical: Two cargo planes with humanitarian aid were dispatched to Sri Lanka and another three, of the AECI and the Red Cross, were dispatched to Sumatra and Thailand. The Government announced a debt moratorium for affected countries. Prime Minister José Luis Rodríguez Zapatero ordered the immediate deployment of a military force to assist in humanitarian tasks, comprising 650 troops, 5 planes with humanitarian aid, 2 helicopters and a hospital-ship in Sumatra. The military mission lasted two months and cost EUR 6.5m.

SWEDEN

SEK 500m ($75m) distributed through SIDA, the Swedish International Development Agency.
Practical: An extensive relief effort on behalf of the government was launched with military personnel, forensic teams and search and rescue teams.
Acts of Charity: As Sweden was probably the nation which, although not directly affected by the Tsunami, was nevertheless the hardest hit, the Swedish public gave generously — about SEK 500m ($75m) — as well as materials such as clothes and other equipment.

SWITZERLAND

Financial: Government allocated CHF 27m ($23.8m).
Practical: Four teams of the Swiss Humanitarian Aid Unit (SHA) deployed in India, Sri Lanka and Thailand. Another team of SHA and WHO doctors and logisticians on the Maldives. Three Super Puma helicopters and 50 personnel sent to Sumatra under the guidance of the UNHCR. Various relief organisations contributed CHF 1m.
Acts of charity: Ongoing appeal for donations organised by 'Swiss Solidarity' resulted in CHF 160m being collected.

SYRIA

Practical: A Syrian aeroplane loaded with 40 tonnes of medical and food aid was dispatched to Indonesia Thursday. Syria's Health Minister, Maher al-Hussami, said the load included 20 tonnes of medicine, food and drinking water, as well as 880 blankets

Acts of Charity: With private philanthropic donations, relief aid from Taiwan was estimated at $60m.

TONGA
Financial: The government pledged $65,000.
Acts of Charity: The Tongan public donated TOP 22,887.

TURKEY
Financial: Turkey donated TRY 28.9m ($37.6m) to be allocated to Sri Lanka, India, Indonesia, Thailand, Malaysia and Maldives and used for construction.

UNITED KINGDOM
Financial: The UK government announced an increase in its aid to GDP 75m on January 10, 2005, up from the GDP 50m ($96m) pledged on December 30, 2004, and the initial pledge of GBP 15m of aid in the early stages. The government also promised to match the public donation. Chancellor of the Exchequer Gordon Brown pushed for the suspension of debt repayments to the industrialised nations.
Practical: The government sent the Royal Fleet Auxiliary ship *RFA Diligence*, the Royal Navy frigate HMS Chatham with Lynx helicopters to move supplies, plus a RAF C-17 Globemaster III and a Tristar strategic airlifter.
Acts of Charity: The people of the UK responded by donating at a rate of up to GBP 1million per hour in the first week of the appeal. At the beginning of 2005, the total raised and given by UK citizens stood at GBP 100m ($190m). On February 26, 2005, it was announced that the Disasters Emergency Committee (an umbrella organisation of 12 aid agencies) was closing its appeal after raising a total of GBP 300m in the two months since the disaster struck. Other British charities raised a total of GBP 50m. Large donations were also made by HM The Queen and other notable

celebrities and wealthy individuals. Half of the FTSE 100 companies announced sizable donations of money and resources, with many other companies donating their services at no cost.

VANUATU (SW PACIFIC)
Financial: The Government contributed VUV 5,000,000 ($47,300) to relief efforts.
Acts of Charity: A benefit concert on January 8, 2005, raised VUV 200,000 ($1,800) for the Vanuatu Red Cross Society.

UNITED STATES
Financial: The United States government immediately allocated $400,000 (GBP 200,000, EUR 300,000) to India, Indonesia, the Maldives and Sri Lanka. Officials worked on a $4m aid package to help the Red Cross. It also prepared an initial $15 million (GBP 8m) aid package for affected nations. An additional $20m (GBP 11m) offered as an emergency line of credit. Aid was later raised to $350m (GBP 190m, EUR 260m).
Practical: Dispatched disaster teams to aid the nations affected and numerous C-5 Galaxy and C-17 Globemaster III strategic airlifters, ten C-130 Hercules tactical airlifters containing disaster supplies, nine P-3C Orion maritime patrol aircraft for search and rescue support, and several teams from the Departments of State and Defense to co-ordinate additional assistance. Offered assistance from its troops stationed in Japan. *USS Abraham Lincoln* aircraft carrier battle group, which was in port in Hong Kong, was dispatched to the coast of Sumatra to provide support to the Indonesian province of Aceh. An amphibious battle group led by *USS Bonhomme Richard*, scheduled for a port call in Guam, were dispatched to render assistance. A total of 48 Navy and Marine Corps helicopters were involved. The US Navy also deployed the *USNS Mercy*, a 1,000-bed hospital ship (to be initially staffed to support 250 patient beds).

More than 12,600 Department of Defense personnel were involved in the relief effort, Operation Unified Assistance.

Acts of Charity: US-based relief groups and non-governmental organisations reported having raised over $515m. One charity said online pledges arrived at a rate of $100,000 an hour. Big corporations such as Coca-Cola and Johnson & Johnson all gave. Hollywood celebrities also donated, including Steven Spielberg ($1.5m) and Sandra Bullock ($1m). US President George W Bush donated $16,000 from his personal funds. The city of Fargo, North Dakota, gave $10,000 of taxpayer money. Motorists in Chattanooga, Tennessee, were allowed to donate money to the relief effort in place of paying for traffic citations. President Bush also called for a nationwide fund raising drive, headed by former US Presidents George H. W. Bush and Bill Clinton.

Below: *U.S. President George W. Bush stands in the middle as former President George H. Bush passes the pen to former President Bill Clinton as they sign a book of condolences at the Indian Embassy in Washington, January 3, 2005.*

Nation By Nation, The Rush To Give

Country	Population (July 2004 or earlier)	Aid (total) (USD millions)	Per capita (USD)
Australia	19,913,144	1,322	66.38
Norway	4,574,560	265.1	57.95
Kuwait	2,257,549	100	44.3
Liechtenstein	32,528	1.2	36.89
Netherlands	16,318,199	509.1	31.20
Ireland	3,939,558	117.94	29.94
Qatar	840,290	20	23.80
Canada	32,507,874	743.68	22.88
Switzerland	7,450,867	157.9	21.19
Sweden	9,010,627	177.2	19.67
Finland	5,214,512	89.5	17.16
Denmark	5,413,392	87.5	16.16
United Kingdom	60,270,708	795.7	13.20
Germany	82,424,609	992	12.04
Iceland	293,966	2.5	8.50
United Arab Emirates	2,523,915	20	7.92
United States	293,027,571	1891	6.45
Japan	127,333,002	580	4.55
Singapore	4,353,893	15	3.45
Belgium	10,348,276	24.9	2.41
Italy	58,057,477	125	2.15
Greece	10,647,529	21.6	2.03
Czech Republic	10,246,178	19	1.85
Spain	40,280,780	73.1	1.81
Saudi Arabia	25,795,938	30	1.16
Portugal	10,524,145	10.9	1.04
France	60,424,213	57	0.94
China	1,298,847,624	63	0.05
Hong Kong (SAR China)	6,855,125	78.2	11.41
India	1,065,070,607	23	0.02

AT THE HEART OF IT ALL

From a small tin in a little school to a mega-dollar event in a huge stadium, fund-raising for the victims and countries left devastated by the Tsunami reached unprecedented limits. While the ordinary man in the street organised collections in offices, shops, restaurants and clubs, others ran marathons and embarked on other challenging sponsored events. The word 'Tsunami' entered the vocabulary of the very young as they were taught the full meaning of this natural disaster — and gave pocket money to all those children in a far off land.

Politicians, millionaire moguls and those from the world of song, showbusiness and sport all made contributions to the Tsunami disaster fund in one way or another. The response for financial aid cut across all countries, creed and colour. At the peak of the fund-raising, no-one it seemed, had failed to give. Or to send up a prayer.

Charity may begin at home, but in the case of the Tsunami Relief Fund 2004-2005, it ended up thousands of miles away helping people whose plight touched the hearts of us all...

In February 2005, former US Presidents George H W Bush and Bill Clinton visited Tsunami-stricken Thailand. At the shattered village of Ban Nam Khem, children who lost family members in the Tsunami presented them with drawings, one showing a giant wave and a rescue helicopter and the other of floodwaters sweeping away people, cars and boats. Bush and Clinton also visited a memorial wall honoring foreign tourists who died, and then dined with Thai Prime Minister Thaksin Shinawatra. Said Bush: "I don't think there's ever been a tragedy that affected the heartbeat of the American people as much as this Tsunami has done. I don't think you can put a limit on it. It's so devastating. They're still finding wreckage, still actually some bodies being recovered."

The two ex-Presidents had been asked by current president George W. Bush to lead the US effort to provide private aid to hundreds of thousands of Tsunami victims. Also on their itinerary of mercy visits were Indonesia, Sri Lanka and the Maldives.

Bill Clinton said an estimated one-third of American households had contributed to Tsunami relief and that governments and private individuals had committed $7 billion to Tsunami relief in Asia, and another $4 billion was needed for a reconstruction process that could take two years.

America's entertainment giants were not slow in contributing to the fund-raising efforts. Country singer Willie Nelson and many other musicians performed a benefit concert and released *Willie Nelson - Songs for Tsunami Relief* From Austin to South Asia. Proceeds went to CARE and UNICEF.

American TV shows *Entertainment Tonight*, *The Early Show* and *The Insider* joined forces with UNICEF to "raise money and awareness" for Tsunami-affected countries. Clay Aiken was the first to join the all-star effort, through a series of public service announcements airing on *ET* and *The Insider*. He said: "It's not a situation where we have to feel helpless. We can actually help out. We continue to see the death toll rising on the news, but I think the biggest story and the biggest need is to help those survivors continue to survive and get back to their normal lives."

Actress Alyssa Milano, a national ambassador for UNICEF, told the shows: "There is no reason to be a celebrity if I can't make positive changes in the world. We can never forget. We have to come together and make the world a better place. That's the incredible experience that we will all learn from this, is what we do, I think, innately as human beings. We want to make things better and we want to stop human suffering."

Actors Leonardo DiCaprio and Sandra Bullock donated large sums to the relief effort. Said Jay Leno: "When Hollywood unites it's a powerful fundraising force." Talk show host Oprah Winfrey launched Oprah Winfrey's Angel Network fund for Tsunami victims.

Jazz stars such as the legendary World Saxophone Quartet, featuring David Murray, Hamlet, Bluiett, Oliver Lake and Bruce Williams, performed a "Salute to Jimi Hendrix" concert in March 2005 in Pittsfield to

Above: *Eric Clapton performs during the Tsunami Relief Concert at the Millennium Stadium in Cardiff, South Wales, January 22, 2005.*

raise funds for long-term housing in Sri Lanka.

Across the Canadian border, a benefit concert in British Columbia on January 13, 2005, included such performers as Tom Cochrane, Blue Rodeo, Bryan Adams, Anne Murray, Rush, Molly Johnson, Oscar Peterson, Jann Arden, Barenaked Ladies, Bruce Cockburn and, in a special segment direct from her Las Vegas stage venue, Céline Dion. Other celebrities included author Margaret Atwood and sports commentator Don Cherry.

Also in Canada, artistes Avril Lavigne, Sum 41 and Sarah McLachlan were among the line-up lined up for a brace of charity concerts in Calgary and Vancouver.

In January 22, 2005, Great Britain held its biggest charity concert since Live Aid, 20 years previously. Tsunami Relief Cardiff was held at the Millennium Stadium in Cardiff, Wales, and raised £1.25million ($1.8m). More than 60,000 people watched the seven-hour event live with millions of others watching from around the world. Those performing included

Eric Clapton, Jools Holland, Lulu, Feeder, Charlotte Church and Midge Ure. Classical singer Katherine Jenkins, opened the show with *Amazing Grace*, *Caruso* and *You'll Never Walk Alone* as the audience waved torches to represent victims of the disaster.

UK Charitable Aid was another British event to raise funds for the Tsunami victims. It consisted of a 12-hour radio show broadcast on 268 radio stations and had an audience of over 20 million covering all of the UK's commercial and national stations as well as student and hospital stations and some overseas ones such as British Forces Broadcasting. Singers who sang live in the studio included Jamie Cullum, Liam Gallagher, David Gray, Jamelia, Texas, Ronan Keating, Bryan Adams, Il Divo, Melanie C, and Russell Watson. Also, British celebrities and leading figures donated items to be auctioned on internet selling and buying site, eBay. Prime Minister Tony Blair donated a guide of 10 Downing Street. The event raised more than £3million.

Meanwhile, DJ Mike Read lined up Band Aid veteran Boy George and pop musician Cliff Richard to record a benefit version of Read's *Grief Never Grows*

AT THE HEART OF IT ALL

Left: *Pop artist Rain (C) of South Korea performs at the MTV Asia Aid benefit concert in Bangkok, February 3, 2005. The concert was attended by both Asian and Western pop stars.*

Old. And young pop star Katie Melua, an ambassador for Save the Children, visited Sri Lanka to see how the charity helped the country recover. She dyed her hands blue to leave a palm print on a book, together with hundreds of Sri Lankans. Said Katie, who also appeared in a fund-raising video: "I love the concept of the video and the book. There are already hand prints from fishermen, children and mothers from all over Sri Lanka. I hope this raised even more money for the great projects that Save the Children have here."

Such visits were a great morale boost to those caught up in the Tsunami. Said 12-year-old Vanathan Prahalathyan: "I can't believe people so far away care so much about us. I don't even know where England is. What they have done is good and kind. After what happened the day after Christmas, I had given up and did not have any hope."

Hong Kong's Hollywood action-movie hero Jackie Chan led a goodwill visit by international celebrities to stricken Tsunami communities. Chan joined fellow Hong Kong film star Eric Tsang, Miss World 2004 Julia Garcia Mantilla and British Olympic gold medalist Daley Thompson on a four-day awareness-raising trip to Sumatra's Aceh region.

After a visit to the affected regions, Latin America singer Ricky Martin teamed up with Habitat for Humanity to build and restore an initial 224 houses as part of a more extensive project in Phang Nga province, Thailand. The singer's Ricky Martin Foundation aimed to help more than 1,000 people move out of temporary shelters or overcrowded camps. Martin visited Thailand shortly after the Tsunami and told reporters: "After looking at those images on television, it was impossible for me to stay at home with my arms crossed."

A one-day international match between Asia and the Rest of the World at the Melbourne Cricket Ground in January raised $Aust 11 million.

Indian star batsman Sachin Tendulkar agreed to play in the Asia XI in a charity game against the International XI at London's famous cricket ground The Oval, on June 20, 2005. Other big names joined

Above: *The singer Ricky Martin entertains children at an orphanage in Bangkok, Thailand.*

him including team-mate Rahul Dravid, Sri Lanka left-arm quick Chaminda Vaas, Pakistan fast bowler Mohammad Sami, Lankan spin great Muttiah Muralitharan India spinners Harbhajan Singh and Anil Kumble and Pakistan all-rounder Azhar Mahmood. The International XI included such names as Australia leg-spin legend Shane Warne, West Indies batting great Brian Lara, South Africa stars Shaun Pollock and skipper Graeme Smith, Kiwi duo Stephen Fleming and Chris Cairns, as well as Surrey and England batsmen Graham Thorpe and Mark Butcher. The event raised money for Tsunami victims in Sri Lanka. Said a delighted Paul Sheldon, chief executive of Surrey County Cricket Club: "Sachin Tendulkar is the biggest name in world cricket, and to have him on the team sheet ensures we reach our target of over £1million for the Oval Cricket Relief Trust."

The Oval Cricket Relief Trust was set up with the intention of donating money to the rebuilding of a village in Sri Lanka, helping with the efforts in Grenada after the hurricanes in 2004 and being able to put money to one side in order to help with the next natural disaster 'in a cricket loving part of the world'.

In April 2005, Actress Konkona Sen joined other Indian celebrities at a charity fashion show to raise money for orphans in the Tsunami-affected areas in India. Singer Shaan staged a musical show in the Tsunami-ravaged Andaman and Nicobar Islands and Bollywood actors including Vivek Oberoi and Rahul Bose also joined in with the relief work of India.

In Norway, dozens of benefit concerts were

Previous page: *Bollywood stars gather on stage after a concert called "HELP" in Bombay on February 6, 2005 to raise funds for Indian tsunami victims.*

organised. In its oil-capital, Stavanger, rock groups organised a free show with cash to be raised through the sail of a single *The Time Is Now*. Said popular Norwegian bluesman Reidar Larsen: "It's about solidarity with people. If you have the chance to help people in need, most will turn out, whether auto mechanics or artists."

Finnish rock stars held a fund-raising concert at one of Helsinki's most popular halls, collecting money for the Red Cross crisis fund. Danish names like rising pop star Tue West and rappers Jokeren and Nik & Jay took part in a day-long telethon in Denmark.

Hong Kong star Nicholas Tse sang *Chinese People* to 6,000 people who waved glow sticks, clapped and sang along at a charity concert at the Workers' Gymnasium in Beijing, and Hong Kong pop legend Andy Lau and other stars took part in fund-raiser that netted more than $6.2 million.

German punk rockers Die Toten Hosen donated proceeds from a concert in Berlin to Doctors without Borders, raising $200,000 from concertgoers and radio listeners and proceeds from an annual benefit concert hosted by German President Horst Koehler at the Berlin Philharmonic all went to Tsunami victims.

A day of concerts featuring French music celebrities was held in Paris and proceeds went to the red Cross.

Some artistes simply gave without performing. The Vienna Philharmonic Orchestra promised a donation of $136,000 to the World Health Organization to help provide drinking water to Tsunami survivors.

Right top: *Tsunami benefit 'Concert on the lake' in New Zealand.*

Right bottom: *Tsunami benefit concert of traditional Indian music Dresden, Germany.*

Below: *Jaycee Fong (C), son of Hong Kong action movie star Jackie Chan, stands beside popular Taiwanese television hostess Chang Hsiao-yen (2nd-R) and other hosts from China and Taiwan*

THE AFTERMATH

Months later, people were still feeling the effect of the day their lives seemed to stand still. Their plight was not helped when a second earthquake hit South-east Asia. Thousands fled their homes in panic on March 28 , 2005, when the earthquake rumbled its mighty roar.

Dozens of people died when buildings collapsed on Nias, the little island 80 miles off Sumatra which had already suffered near destruction from the Boxing Day Tsunami. The nearby islands of Simeulue and Banyak also lost buildings and roads. The quake, measuring 8.7, struck on the same fault line. Its epicenter was 19 miles underground, 125 miles west north-west of Sibolga in Sumatra, between Nias and Simeulue.

In April, Indonesia's Disaster Management Agency reported that the death toll throughout the area had risen to 714. "There will be more," Giri Trigono, an official at the agency, told Reuters news agency, adding that more than 140,000 people had been left homeless as a result of the March earthquake.

It was yet another challenge to relief organisations, the United Nations and military personnel from countries including Australia and the United States, who were already fighting an uphill battle from the December Tsunami. The damage to roads and other infrastructure made reaching isolated communities difficult and many people were still sleeping in tents because of regular aftershocks. Other islanders were yet to return from the hills where they had fled fearing a second tsunami as devastating as the first.

The shocks of the March quake were felt as far away as the Malaysian capital of Kuala Lumpur, more than 300 miles distant, and Bangkok, where people living in high rises made a dash for open ground.

The December earthquake was around 200 miles further north, and experts said the March tremor was an 'aftershock'. But there were widespread fears that it would trigger another tsunami, and coastal areas of Indonesia, Thailand and Sri Lanka were evacuated amid scenes of terror.

With the earth seeming to conspire against them, the people of South East Asia wondered if life would ever be the same again. Children, especially, were badly emotionally scarred. Eight-year-old

> "He's still really scared. Whenever there's a rumour about another wave, he runs away and doesn't come back for ages."
>
> Thoon Navarak, father of eight-year-old Anasorn, who survived the first earthquake and Tsunami.

Anasorn Navarak fled to the hills the day the second earthquake threatened to hit Thailand.

There were good reasons for his fears. Anasorn survived the December Tsunami by floating on a piece of wood. He climbed into a tree but when the water went down again he had to wait several hours before he was rescued. "It's not something he can just forget," said his father, Thoon Navarak.

To help little ones like Anasorn, by the time the second tsunami hit, children's centers had been set up in refugee camps, trained psychologists had been brought in to counsel those who had lost loved ones, and school teachers had begun to regain the trust of pupils whose lives had been turned upside down.

Thavich Jitprasarn, the director of a primary school in Baan Nam Khem, one of the Thai villages worst hit by the Boxing Day Tsunami, said only time would ease the pain. "Children move on very quickly but many of them still don't really want to talk about what happened. The older children, especially, are finding it difficult to cope."

The school was badly damaged and after the disaster, pupils were taught in the open air. Out of the 419 children who attended the school, 27 died. Almost every pupil had lost a friend. Seven lost their parents.

Outside of school hours, aid agencies at the refugee children's centers, worked hard to bring some air of normality into shattered lives. "With the little children, we spend time singing and painting, but with older children, we just talk to them about their problems," said Phakamas Kamcham, a staff member in Thaptawan camp. "They are getting over it. But they will never forget."

Many, it seems will never forget the day the devil wave reached out of the sea. Said one mother, Songdao Ponkaen, of her three-year-old son Charnathip: "He still has nightmares about the Tsunami. When we got back home after it, he ran in

> **"The little ones don't understand everything fully, but maybe when they grow up they will feel sad for the people they have lost."**
>
> **Thavich Jitprasarn, director of the primary school in Baan Nam Khem, Thailand**

to what remained of our house and, before we could stop him, he saw the dead bodies of his cousin and his uncle. Only yesterday, he asked if the Tsunami was coming back..."

Those who survived Thailand's December Tsunami still felt their lives were lost in other ways. No-one was exempt from the fear. "I'm afraid, I'm so afraid of another tsunami," said Chulin Promdeng, 42, a masseuse. "For 15 days, I didn't sleep. I keep looking for another tsunami."

Months later, beaches normally packed with tourists were deserted. So too were dive shops, hotels and restaurants. Much needed livelihoods to help the survivors envisage a brighter future were hard to achieve. One resident, Yew Sittipan who ran a thriving souvenir stand before the Tsunami struck, could only hang his head in despair. "Normally my shop is really full at this time, because it's high season. Now hardly anyone comes. We've already had Sars and bird flu in Thailand, and now this. What else is there to come?".

Other prime holiday areas of the sunshine idyll were slowly picking up, however. Patong, the main

Below: *Houses in a village on the eastern coastline of the Ampara region of Sri Lanka lie destroyed after being hit by the Tsunami. Torrential rains flooded parts of coastal eastern Sri Lanka, cutting off roads being used for vital relief.*

tourist strip on the island of Phuket, was one off the most successful at attracting holidaymakers back to its beaches. Three months on, its main road, full of bars and restaurants, looked almost as crowded as usual.

Indeed, Phuket, the tourist jewel in Thailand's crown, made a remarkable recovery, with almost one hundred per cent business as usual by the end of April 2005. Amongst the items on sale were commemorative T-shirts bearing the words "Patong Beach, Phuket, Thailand. 2001 Bomb Alert, 2002 SARS, 2003 Bird Flu, 2004 Tsunami — What's Next?"

Hotels, however, were not immediately able to attract custom as before, with only seven to ten per cent occupancy — hardly surprising when about 40

Below: *A statue of Buddha laying among the ruins of a collapsed temple on the coast road near the village of Hikkaduwa, southern Sri Lanka, January 13, 2005.*

"Gunung Sitoli is now like a dead town. The situation here is in extreme panic."
Mayor of Gunung Sitoli, the main town of Nias, on Sumatra.

per cent of the 53,000 hotel rooms available in six southern provinces were destroyed by the tsunami. Before the tragedy, around 300,000 tourists visited Phuket every month. In February, 2005, that number was down to 37,813. I

"People say, 'How can you go to Thailand? It's dangerous'," Louis Bronner, general manager of Mom Tri's Boathouse hotel, told the *New York Herald Tribune*. "Weeks after the Tsunami, they still think there are bodies floating, fish contaminated, polluted water, and that you can get cholera, typhoid, crazy things like this."

As occupancy dropped, some hotels gave their employees only three weeks' pay for a month's work.

Others sent their workers out to trawl the beaches with fliers offering deep cuts in rates.

Some potential visitors held back, particularly in the early days, out of a sense that it would be unseemly to splash in the surf in a place of death and mourning. Said one, 51-year-old Briton Gordon Brind: "You do think about that. It's sad when you look out at the sea and how it looks now and you think of all the death out there. It's on your mind."

Phuket was still far less affected than the newly-opened resorts of Khao Lak, about 65 kilometers to the north were official reports said 80 per cent of the buildings were destroyed. Months after the Tsunami hit, huge resort complexes, some of them still under construction when the waves hit, were vast dirt lots, their buildings in ruins, many of their workers and

Below: *A bird's eye view of the eroded shore line at Kachal island of the Andaman and Nicobar island chains in this picture taken December 28, 2004.*

guests swept out to sea.

But slowly, slowly, the Thai people were putting their world back together. "I think the Thais have done really well," said British tourist Sarah McKay. "When you're in the bars here you almost forget that the Tsunami happened. It's only when you go down to the beach that you see the damage"

There was one type of excursion which proved to be popular, particularly in Phuket — tourists hiring taxis and buses to travel to the areas worst hit by the disaster. Lars Schmidt, a Danish tourist in Phuket, explained: "When we heard on the news what happened, we wanted to see it for ourselves. I'd been to Khao Lak before the Tsunami so I just wanted to see what had happened." A police boat that was washed several kilometers inland by the Tsunami, and had come to rest in a group of trees, was also a popular sight for visitors. "It's becoming a tourist attraction," said Karen Blackman, a British volunteer in Khao Lak. "There are plans to leave it as a memorial." Ms

> "When someone asks me about my sisters, I say they are staying with family somewhere else. I don't want them to know what really happened."
>
> Shantini, 14, Sri Lankan girl who lost both her sisters.

Right top: *An aerial view of Khao Lak, about 115 km (72 miles) north of the Thai island of Phuket, December 30, 2004.*

Right bottom: *Indonesian residents of Lhokseumawe, in northern Sumatra's Aceh province, struggle through flood water.*

Blackman set up a shop close to the police boat, selling products made by victims of the Tsunami.

However, throughout much of the region, the lingering, pitiful plight of many Tsunami victims reduced tourists to tears — as, with the passage of time, their thread of hope for lost loved ones became thinner and thinner.

As Eric Lipton wrote of Sumatra in the New York Times: "In Aceh Province, the destruction has been so profound, with more than 100,000 thought to be dead and with mass graves making identification difficult, that a missing persons list, like the one spontaneously started in the hours after the World Trade Center attack in New York, makes no practical sense. For this suffering city, the 'Alive' list has had to do, as a focal point of the effort to reunite families."

Said Natalie Klein of the International Committee of the Red Cross: "The cold truth is that if people are missing without a trace, it means they are dead. In that environment, a list of the living is the only option."

Survivors in Sumatra who had been separated from relatives were asked to fill out a one-page form with their name, age, sex, place of residence before the disaster and their temporary new address. The Red Cross also offered free satellite telephone calls to victims. Within a few days, around 800 "I'm Alive" names were posted on a bulletin board on the main Red Cross office based in a Toyota car showroom. An "I am Alive Book" was distributed to homeless camps and Red Cross offices across the region.

Many thousands of stories did not have a happy ending. Clothing vendor Amiruddin, 38, tried to find his wife and three children in the neighbourhood where he once lived. Nothing remains there except for the foundations of what used to be people's homes. "I have no words to express it," he said. "I have nobody. No wife, no children. May God help. I have faith."

Volunteers who had been working tirelessly on the relief effort were not spared their own grief. Suci Lestari Gunawan, 22, a field officer in the Banda Aceh branch of the Red Cross, was unable to find 26 members of her family. The day before the earthquake, almost all of them had gathered at her home to celebrate the pending departure of her grandmother for a religious pilgrimage. The house was destroyed and Ms.Gunawan had no idea what happened to her grandmother, mother, brother, sister and more than a dozen aunts and uncles. Her father, who was out fishing when the Tsunami hit, miraculously survived. Other family members could not be traced.

Said Ms.Gunawan: "Even if it is a million to one chance, I believe in it. There is hope. But it is just so very, very sad. This disaster has changed us all forever."

Reporting from Banda Aceh, Tyler Hicks of *The New York Times* made some tragic observations. At one point in the rescue operation, recovery teams were finding more than 2,000 bodies a day. Hicks wrote:

"Ramza, the body searcher, apologised to the dead man, in terrible shape, as he prised him out of the truck's crushed cabin, 'This may hurt'. Nearby lay three other bodies — skeletons, really, after so much time in the sun and rain — already wrapped in plastic. Mr. Ramza, 24, and his crew found two more bodies in the hour before quitting time, for a total of some 35 in one small section, maybe 100 yards square, of this devastated city.

"All around Aceh Province that day, 1,438 new bodies were picked from where they lay, then counted and buried. Almost a month after the Tsunami hit, huge numbers of bodies are still being found here, a reminder that for all the money and outside help, even the most basic condition for a return to normalcy is nowhere near.

"On Monday, searchers found 2,440 bodies. Two

days before, the number was 2,972. For the first time, the numbers have now dropped below 2,000 a day, though not because the dead are close to being cleared. It is just harder to get to them now."

The Indonesian government's aim to pick up all bodies by January 26, 2005, was a seemingly futile one. Rescuers believed at least 10,000 more bodies were scattered under collapsed houses, crushed into mud and tons of debris.

Budi Almadi Adiputro, the day-to-day chief of the Indonesian National Co-ordinating Board of Disaster Management, had a gruesome statement to make: "In the first week, the smell was not so bad. With a simple mask and simple gloves, they could handle it. But after two weeks, three weeks... If you talk about the dead, it is only an estimation. God always gives us miracles — who knows?"

Around 1.8 million people in Aceh lost their jobs and livelihoods as a result of the Tsunami. About 38 per cent of the total population of Aceh and North Sumatra moved deeper into poverty, as local unemployment rates rose to 30 per cent or higher in some areas. On the positive side for Indonesia, however, it was hoped that massive reconstruction programmes would lead to the restoration of at least half of all jobs lost and the recovery of up to 85 per cent of all jobs within 24 months of the disaster.

Humanitarian group World Vision began to develop livelihood recovery projects in Aceh, targeting an initial group of families who have returned to their original communities but have no work. The group provided fishing boats in an effort to help the homeless start to earn a living.

Together with its immediate construction of temporary living centres for those who lost their homes, World Vision hoped to supply 80 TLCs (Temporary Location Centres), each supplied with water and sanitation, schools and other services. Contracts drawn up for the TLCs stipulated that they can eventually be dismantled by the homeless if the materials are used for construction and repair of their homes.

Other problems hindered emotional and practical recovery. As in the case of the children of the Tender Sprouts orphanage at Puthukkudiyiruppu, in Tamil-controlled north-eastern Sri Lanka. Many of the children were orphaned during the long years of civil war between the Tamil Tigers and the Sri Lankan government. The Tender Sprouts orphanage was the third premises they had had to move to, their last one having been swept away by the Tsunami. Helpers had a tough job on their hands trying to let the children know that life could hold some hope for them. Said one Tender Sprouts co-ordinator: "Many of the children still cry at night or wake up with bad dreams. And they are all now scared of the sea."

In March, a survey conducted by the Medical Research Institute in co-operation with WFP and UNICEF found that stunting and wasting in Sr Lankan camps was 3.4 per cent above average, exacerbated by post-Tsunami conditions. In response, World Vision, WFP and the Sri Lanka Government signed an agreement which enabled supplementary feeding for children in affected districts.

As well as heavy toll on human lives, the events of Boxing Day 2004 caused an enormous environmental impact that will affect South East Asia for many years to come. Severe damage was inflicted on ecosystems, such as mangroves, coral reefs, forests, coastal wetlands, vegetation, sand dunes and rock formations, animal and plant biodiversity and groundwater.

One of the most devastating effects on the areas was the poisoning of the fresh water supplies and the soil by salt water infiltration and deposit of a salt layer over arable land. At one point, 17 coral reef atolls in the Maldives that had been overcome by sea waves were totally without fresh water. They could be rendered uninhabitable for decades. In response to a request from the Maldivian Government, the Australian Government sent ecological experts to help restore the marine environments and coral reefs — the lifeblood of Maldivian tourism. Much of the ecological expertise has been rendered from work with the Great Barrier Reef, in Australia's north-eastern waters.

An uncountable number of wells that served communities were invaded by sea, sand and earth, and aquifers were invaded through porous rock. Salted-over soil becomes sterile, and it is difficult and costly to restore for agriculture.

Previous page: *Aerial view of damaged Indian Air force mess hall at tsunami-devastated Car Nicobar island in the southern part of the Indian Andamans and Nicobar archipelago, January 10, 2005.*

It also causes the death of plants and important soil micro-organisms. Thousands of rice, mango and banana plantations in Sri Lanka were destroyed almost entirely and will take years to recover.

In addition, the spread of solid and liquid waste and industrial chemicals, water pollution and the destruction of sewage collectors and treatment plants threatened the environment even further, in untold ways. The environmental impact will take a long time and significant resources to assess.

There were crucial lessons to be learned from the Tsunami tragedy — both in how to prevent an event of such destructive magnitude from ever happening again, to how the world should deal with such a disaster. On January 26, 2005, Barbara Stocking, Director of OXFAM Great Britain, issued a statement:

"The response of the world to the Tsunami has been impressive but important lessons need to be learnt... Despite the scale of the response, the crisis has bought with it real challenges that remain. In particular, it calls on those co-ordinating the response to ensure

Below: *A main village road, near a statue of Mahatma Gandhi, is blocked by debris in Malika, Car Nicobar after the Tsunami hit the remote Andaman and Nicobar islands chain, near the epicenter of the quake.*

that all agencies working in the region are appropriate to the task. In some cases, the influx of money has meant that there are too many organisations working without the appropriate experience, competencies and skills... Aid agencies are also urged to do more to consult with the communities they are there to help. A lack of consultation has meant that some of the aid delivered has not always been what is most needed. For example, in Sri Lanka, some of the housing is being built without consultation and is not appropriate. Donors and those co-ordinating the response need to ensure that all agencies are working to meet the internationally accepted 'Sphere' standards for disaster relief.

"One month ago, the world responded to the Tsunami with an unprecedented aid effort. Oxfam too launched a global response and is already helping over 300,000 people. Undoubtedly this work has saved lives, but there are many challenges that cannot be ignored. The amount of money raised means that governments and aid agencies must address issues of the quality, not just quantity of aid.

"The issues of conflict, debt and trade have not yet been adequately addressed by the international community. Unless they are, the victims of the Tsunami will never escape poverty."

In the months following the Tsunami, debate raged over how to prevent a repeat of the catastrophe. This seemed heartbreakingly simple. An early-warning system was needed for, although seismologists knew almost immediately about the earthquake off Indonesia that triggered the Tsunami, there was no way of relaying that information to people in the region.

In April 2005, Asian and African leaders agreed to establish a 'multi nodal tsunami warning network' to prevent a repeat of the total devastation and carnage it had suffered. Plans for the system, which would see warning centres established across Asia and Africa, were endorsed by 89 heads of state, ministers and officials from both continents at a two-day summit in the Indonesian capital of Jakarta.

"We are determined to establish an integrated strategy for the development of a multi-nodal early warning system with mechanisms for preparedness, prevention, mitigation and response, with a view to minimizing casualties," the leaders said in the statement. "We are determined that, harnessed within a spirit of compassion, sacrifice and endurance, our preparedness and capacity to pro actively address the effects of tsunami, earthquake and other natural disasters will prevail."

The $30 million system included a number of deep water measuring devices on the ocean floor which would relay wave movements to surface buoys and then to a satellite. That information and data from an extended network of tide gauges would be collated at a new Indian Ocean tsunami centre. It is up to each individual country to take appropriate action when they get warnings. It was hoped it would be up and running for the Indian Ocean by June 2006 and that a global system would follow a year later.

UNESCO head Koichiro Matsuura said the $30 million was a small price to pay after events of December 2004. "It's peanuts compared to what happened," he said. "We learned this in a very costly way."

Later that same month, a series of beach guard lookout towers were authorised for the coast around Phuket. Others were planned for Andaman province. The lookout posts, operating independently of the National Disaster Warning Center alarm system, would, according to the *Phuket Gazette*: "Enable beach guards to monitor the sea for signs of tsunamis, as well as watch out for other problems such as drownings or boat sinkings." The lookout stations were equipped with an alarm system capable of issuing a 105-decibel alert and searchlights with a range of 500 meters. Determined to leave nothing to chance against nature in the future, the guards staffing the stations were trained by the Royal Thai Navy.

The ghosts of the 2004 Tsunami may take forever to lay. During their visits to the affected areas, health professionals and aid workers said local people were witnessing many sightings of ghosts, particularly those of foreigners. In all likelihood, this stemmed from the fact that traditional beliefs in many of the affected regions state that a relative of the family must bury the body of the dead or the ghost will return. It was an after-effect of the Tsunami that many could not have predicted and believed by some experts to be evidence of psychological trauma.

Others felt that what many considered to be the work of the devil was, in fact, a punishment from

THE AFTERMATH

Left top: *Debris is strewn around a village in Phang Nga, north of Phuket, Thailand, January 2, 2005.*

Left bottom: *Workers clear up an area damaged by the Tsunami in Thailand's Phi Phi island, January 3, 2005.*

Below: *A bridge destroyed by the Tsunami is seen through the broken walls of a building in Pottivul, about 85 km (53 miles) south of Kalmunai on Sri Lanka's east coast, January 22, 2005.*

God — retribution for the sex tourist industries of southeast Asia. This rather archaic explanation met with considerable controversy and opposition, especially as the hardest hit area, Aceh, in Sumatra, is considered to be a religiously conservative Islamic society and has had no tourism or Western presence at all in recent years due to armed conflict between the Indonesian military and Acehnese separatists.

Nevertheless, the Boxing Day Tsunami of 2005 will still be remembered as a disaster of Biblical proportions ... and its repercussions felt for many years to come.

THE AFTERMATH

Left: *The scene on a road and a popular boardwalk along the sea that was submerged in Port Blair, the capital of India's Andaman and Nicobar archipelago, January 11, 2005.*

Below: *An Indian fisherman inspects his fishing boat which was brought ashore by the Tsunami in Kanniyakumari, 740 km (463 miles) south from the Indian city of Madras, January 5, 2005.*

THE AFTERMATH

left top: *Indian survivors carry belongings as they leave their houses in Karamawadi village on the outskirts of Nagapattinam, 350 km (219 miles) south of the southern Indian city of Madras, December 27, 2004.*

Left bottom: *A damaged building is seen submerged in water after the Tsunami hit near Malacca jetty in the badly affected Car Nicobar island, located near the southern part of the Indian Andamans and Nicobar archipelago, January 20, 2005.*

Below: *Kalmuni's beach is devastated after the Tsunami hit the Muslim town in eastern Sri Lanka, December 30, 2004.*

Next page: *This aerial view shows a French-owned cement factory at Lhok Nga along the tsunami-battered coast south of Indonesia's Banda Aceh, January 5, 2005.*

Previous page: *A bus is submerged in a flooded area outside Unawatuna, Sri Lanka.*

Right: *Satellite photo showing Tarangambadi.*

Below: *Devastation of Banda Aceh following the Tsunami. Photo taken December 28, 2004.*

TSUNAMI:
THE 'FINAL' TOLL

The most often quoted total of those who perished in the Tsunami is "More than 200,000". The lowest estimate is 190,000, and the highest authoritative estimate is 250,000. But no-one will ever really know the exact number, since tens of thousands still officially listed as 'missing', and over a million have been left homeless.

Tragically, relief agencies reported that one third of those they could confirm as dead were children. This was because of the high proportion of children in the populations of many of the affected regions, plus the fact that children were highly vulnerable targets for the surging water. And international charity Oxfam reported that as many as four times more women than men were killed in some regions because they were waiting on the beach for the fishermen to return or looking after their children at home,.

In addition to the large number of local residents, nationals from more than 50 countries or territories (mostly European tourists) enjoying the peak holiday travel season were among the dead or missing. The European nation hardest hit may have been Sweden, which reported more than 500 dead or missing .

In short, the December 2004 Tsunami was the worst single tsunami in recorded history. Measured in lives lost, the preceding earthquake was one of the worst ten ever.

Here, nation by nation, is a summary of the disaster, death, devastation and lingering tragedy of the affected countries...

INDONESIA

Was seriously affected by both the earthquake and Tsunami which swamped the northern and western coastal areas of Sumatra and its smaller outlying islands. The western tip of the Indonesian island — the closest inhabited area to the epicenter of the earthquake — was devastated. Nearly all the casualties and damage occurred in the province of Aceh, including Leupung and Gleebruk in the Kabupaten/Kota district of Aceh Basar, close to the capital of Banda Aceh, and Teunom in the Aceh Barat (West Aceh) district of Sumatra. Around 800,000 people were left homeless.

Deaths: 131,029 confirmed (possibly 220,000)
Injured: 100,000
Missing: 37,066

Banda Aceh.
Deaths: 30,000
Leupung.
Deaths: 9,000.
Gleebruk.
Deaths unknown.
Completely destroyed.
Teunom.
Deaths: around 8,000.
Area virtually disappeared.
Calan.
Deaths: around 6,000.
Virtually destroyed.
Meulabo.
Deaths: estimated 40,000.
Struck by a series of seven waves which devastated the 120,000 population.
Around 50,000 people lost their homes in the region.
Western Islands: Simeulue.
Deaths: 1 (in earthquake).
Around 90 per cent of buildings destroyed.
Nias.
Deaths: 600 to 1,000

SRI LANKA

Suffered more from the Tsunami than anywhere else apart from Indonesia. Southern and eastern coastlines were the worse hit and badly ravaged. Homes, crops and fishing boats destroyed. Authorities and the Tamil Tigers gave the number of confirmed deaths as 48,677. Many of the dead were children and the elderly.

At Trincomalee in the north east, the Tsunami reached more than two kilometers (1.25 miles) inland and completely submerged the naval base there. About 1,200 dead were counted at Batticaloa in the east. In neighbouring Amparai district alone, more than 5,000 died. About 1,000 more dead were counted in Mullaitivu and Vadamaradchi East.

Sri Lanka suffered the worst single incident when the *Sea Queen* train travelling between Colombo and Galle and carrying 1,600 passengers was struck by a giant tsunami wave at Telwatta and all but 300 were killed. One and a half million people were made homeless and 4,000 people lost their jobs.

On the morning of Thursday December 30, more people were wounded when people fled tsunami affected areas after the Indian government erroneously warned of another possible tsunami.

Deaths: 31,229 confirmed (possibly 39,000)
Injured: 15,686
Missing: 4,093

Batticaloa.
Deaths 1,200
Trincomalee.
Deaths: 800
Amparai.
Deaths 5,000
Mullaitivu and Vadamaradchi East.
Deaths: 1,000.

INDIA

The number of dead was given as 15,493. The south-west coast, especially the state of Tamil Nadu, was the worst affected area on the mainland. At least 7,968 confirmed dead in the mainland province of Tamil Nadu alone, 560 in Pondicherry and around 1,829 of the the 400,000 inhabitants on the islands of Andaman, Nicobar and Katchall.

At least 14,000 Indians, mostly from fishing families were placed in relief centres. Some 2,000 fishing boats lost in Andra Pradesh state and 700 km of road were destroyed.Of the total missing, 4,310 were from Katchall island alone. In what may be the only positive note of the Tsunami, the water washed away centuries of sand from some of the ruins of a 1200-year-old lost city a Mahabalipuram on the south coast.

Deaths: 10, 749 confirmed (possibly 15,500)
Injured: 16,749
Missing: 5,640

Andaman and Nicobar Islands.
Although administered by India, the Andaman and Nicobar Islands are a special case, lying just north of the earthquake epicenter. They comprise 572 islands, out of which 38 are inhabited, both by people from the mainland and indigenous tribes. The Tsunami reached a height of 15 meters in the southern Nicobar Islands. The official death toll was 812, with about 7,000 people missing. The unofficial death toll (including those missing and presumed dead) is estimated to be about 7,000. One fifth of the population of the Nicobar islands were reported dead, injured or missing. The majority of the population of Andaman Islands is made up of people from the mainland, mostly from West Bengal and Tamil Nadu.

Chowra Island.
Lost two thirds of its population of 1,500. Entire islands were washed away, and the island of Trinketsplit in two.

Nancowry group of islands.
Some of the islands were completely submerged and at least 7,000 people lost contact with the outside world when communication systems collapsed.

Andhra Pradesh.
Deaths: 105, made up of 35 from the district of Krishna, 35 from Prakasam, 20 from Nellore, four from Guntur, eight from West Godavari and three from East Godavari.

Kerala.
Deaths: 168, made up from 131 from the district of Kollam, 32 from Alappuzha, and five from Ernakulam.

Pondicherry.
Deaths: 560, made up from 107 from Pondicherry and 453 from Karaikal.

Tamil Nadu.
The state of Tamil Nadu was the the worst affected on the mainland, with a death toll of 7,793. Its state capital Chennai suffered 206 deaths.

Nagapattinam district.

Deaths: 5,525. Entire villages destroyed. The death toll at Velankanni in the Nagapattinam district was around 1,500 alone. Most of these people were visiting the Basilica of the Virgin Mary for Christmas while others were residents of the town. The nuclear power station at Kalpakkam was shut down after sea water rushed into a pump station. About 100 casualties were reported from Kalpakkam, all power plant personnel and their families.

Kanyakumari district.

Deaths 808. Those killed in Kanyakumari included pilgrims taking a holy dip in the sea. Of about 700 people trapped at the Vivekananda Rock Memorial off Kanyakumari, 650 were rescued. In Chennai, people playing on the Marina beach and those who taking a Sunday morning stroll were washed away, in addition to the fisherfolk who lived along the shore and those out at sea.

Cuddalore.

Deaths: 599

Kancheepuram.

Deaths: 124

The death tolls in other districts were Pudukkotai 15, Ramanathapuram 6, Tirunelveli 4, Thoothukudi 3, Tiruvallur 28, Thanjavur 22, Tiruvarur 10 and Viluppuram 47.

THAILAND.

West coast severely hit, including outlying islands and tourist resorts near Phuket. Damage confined to the six southern provinces facing the Andaman Sea. Among more than 5,000 people who died were a significant number of foreigners holidaying in Thailand — over 1,700 from a total of 36 countries. The Thai government originally estimated that 8,000 died but this was amended to a lower figure later. The popular tourist resort of Phuket was badly hit. The smaller but increasingly popular resort area of Khao Lak, some 80 kilomerters north of Phuket, was hit far worse with 3,950 confirmed deaths, while the total amount of dead in Khao Lak probably exceeded 4,500. The severity of the situation in Khao Lak was probably explained by the fact that, unlike the high-rising city of Phuket, the village of Khao Lak only had low-built bungalows instead of high-rise concrete hotels. Khao Lak also has an extensive area of flatland only a few meters above the sea level, on which most bungalows were situated. The high number of deaths included many foreign visitors.

Deaths: 5,395 (approx foreign 2,510)
Injured: 8,457 (Thai 6,065, foreign 2,392)
Missing: 2, 817

Krabi.

Deaths: 686 (Thai 288, foreign 188). Injured: 1,376 (Thai 808, foreign 568).
Missing: 890

Phang Nga.

Deaths: 4,163 (Thai 1,950., foreign 2,213). Injured: 5,597 (Thai 4,344, foreign 1,253).
Missing: 2,113

Phuket.

Deaths: 262 (Thai 154, foreign 105). Injured: 1,111 (Thai 591, foreign 520).
Missing: 700

Ranong.

Deaths: 169 (Thai 167, foreign 2). Injured: 246 (Thai 215, foreign 31).
Missing: 12

Satun.

Deaths: 6 (Thai 0, foreign 6). Injured: 15 (Thai 15, foreign 0).
Missing: 0

Trang.

Deaths: 5 (Thai 3, foreign 2). Injured: 112 (Thai 92, foreign 20).
Missing: 1

THE MALDIVES.

Twenty of the 199 inhabited islands totally destroyed. Greater impact prevented because of the islands' position on the tips of underwater volcanoes.

Deaths: 82
Injured: 108
Missing: 26

Tsunami: The 'Final' Toll

MALAYSIA.

Despite its proximity to the epicenter of the earthquake, Malaysia escaped the kind of damage that struck countries thousands of miles further away because it was shielded by Sumatra. Its worst affected areas were the northern coastal areas and outlying islands like Penang and Langkawi. The simple red flag warning system used by lifeguards on beaches in some resort areas in Penang was credited with reducing the number of fatalities.

Deaths: 68 (made up of 52 in Penang, 12 in Kedah, three in Perak, one in Selangor.
Injured: 74
Missing: 299

MYANMAR.

The worst affected area was the Irrawaddy Delta, inhabited by farmers and fishing families. The military junta put the numbers of dead at 61 but believed to be much higher. As many as 7,000 missing but many thought to have been refugees who fled back to Thailand. Authorities also said that 2,500 Burmese citizens based in Phang Nga, Thailand, had died.

Deaths: 61 confirmed (possibly 90)
Injured: Unknown
Missing: Up to 7,000 unverified

SOMALIA.

Worst-hit African state, with damage concentrated in the region of Puntland, on the tip of the Horn of Africa. As many as 30,000 people lost their homes, around 1,180 homes destroyed and 2,400 boats smashed. Freshwater wells and reservoirs rendered unusable.

Deaths: 298
Injured: 400
Missing: Up to 5,000 unverified

TANZANIA.

Ten people dead. Unknown number missing. Oil tanker ran aground in Dar es Salaam harbour, damaging an oil pipeline.

SOUTH AFRICA.

Two people reported killed — a boy while swimming in the Quinera River at Gonubie, close to East London, and an adult at Blue Horizon Bay, near Port Elizabeth. This was the furthest point from the epicenter of the earthquake that a tsunami-related death was reported. Seven people reported missing. Large concrete blocks were uprooted in East London harbour where boats also broke from their mooring, and boats and cars were submerged at the harbour's Algoa Bay Yacht Club.

BANGLADESH.

Two children killed after a tourist boat capsized.

KENYA.

One person drowned at Watamu near Mombasa.

YEMEN.

One child killed. Forty fishing boats wrecked on Socotra Island.

SEYCHELLES.

Three people dead, seven missing. Major bridge in Port Victoria destroyed.

Such was the force of the earthquake and tsunamis, that several other distant countries suffered damage...

AUSTRALIA.
Tremors were felt along the north-western coast and there was some minor flooding. There were reports that seas off Western Australia surged between Geraldton, 425 kilometers north of Perth, where several boats were ripped from their moorings, and Busselton, 325 kilomerters south of Perth, where a father and a son in a boat were washed out to sea. They were later rescued. Swimmers at Christmas Island were sucked one and a half kilometers out to sea but then brought safely back to shore on the waves.

MADAGASCAR.
Flooding in low-flying coastal districts. Waves reported as being between 1.6 and 10 meters high swept through south eastern coastal areas near the towns of Manakara, Sambava and Vohemar making more than 1,000 people homeless.

MAURITIUS.
Struck by a wave, with one northern village completely submerged. People ignored police warnings to stay off the beach and thronged to watch.

OMAN.
Hit by waves.

SINGAPORE.
Tremors felt by those living in high-rise apartment blocks in the south of the city state.

REUNION (FRENCH).
Serious damage to port infrastructure. Over 200 boats sunk.

Even further afield, the force of the earthquake and Tsunamis was felt by eleven far-flung countries...

AMERICAN SAMOA.
Tsunami energy that passed into the Pacific Ocean caused wave fluctuations of 13cm from crest to trough at Pago Pago.

ANTARCTICA.
Wave fluctuations of 73 cm were detected at Showa Stations 5,000 miles (8,900 km) from the epicenter.

BRAZIL.
Even on the coast of the Atlantic Ocean, the city of Rio de Janeiro detected unusual tidal fluctuations that changed up and down 30cm each half hour — whereas normally it should vary up to 1.3 meters in four hours. In the city of Niteroi, the sea level went up to 60cm and flooded 50 houses belonging to fishermen.

CHILE.
The knock-on affect of the tsunami touched on the Pacific Ocean causing wave fluctuations of 19cm at Iquique

FUJI.
Wave fluctuations of 11cms were recorded in the Pacific Ocean at Suva.

Tsunami: The 'Final' Toll

RUSSIA.

Wave fluctuations of 29cms were recorded on the Pacific Ocean coast of Russia Far East.

MEXICO.

Wave fluctuations of 2.6 meters in the Pacific Ocean at Manzanillo, Colima.

NEW ZEALAND.

Wave fluctuations in the Pacific Ocean of 65cm at Jackson Bay and 50cms at Waitangi on Chatcham Island.

PERU.

Wave fluctuations of 50cm in the Pacific Ocean at Callao.

UNITED STATES.

Wave fluctuations in the Pacific Ocean of 22cm at San Diego, California and 6cm at Hilo, Hawaii.

VANUATU (SW PACIFIC)

Wave fluctuations in the Pacific Ocean of 18 cms at Port Vila.

THE DEATH TOLL AROUND THE WORLD

Few countries were unaffected by the Tsunami. Across the world, in countries far from the immediate tragedy, governments — and individual families — counted the cost in human lives...

ARGENTINA
Two Argentinian nationals died, according to the Ministry of Foreign Affairs.

AUSTRALIA
The number of dead varied greatly, with several hundred Australians at first reported dead, then 30 to 100, and finally 21, with six missing.

AUSTRIA
Confirmed number of 49 dead in Thailand and Sri Lanka and 54 reported missing.

BELGIUM
Ten Belgians confirmed dead in Thailand.

BRAZIL
At first, around 300 people were listed as missing, but most of these were later tracked down and found alive. Brazilian diplomat Lys Amayo de Benedek D'Avola and her ten-year-old son died in Phi, Phi, Thailand.

CANADA
Fifteen Canadians were confirmed dead, including one in Sri Lanka and two in Phuket. Around 12 were injured and seven reported missing.

CHILE
Two dead.

CHINA
Three confirmed dead. Eight were injured in Thailand and 15 missing.

COLOMBIA
An 18-month-old baby was reported dead in Thailand and her parents and brother injured.

CROATIA
A three-year-old girl died in Thailand.

CZECH REPUBLIC
Five confirmed dead — four in Thailand and one in Sri Lanka. Three others missing, presumed dead in Thailand. Five injured, including supermodel Petra Nemcova.

THE DEATH TOLL AROUND THE WORLD

DENMARK

A total of 36 confirmed dead and ten missing. All but two of the dead lost their lives in Thailand.

ESTONIA

Two confirmed dead in Thailand, one missing.

FINLAND

Confirmed 178 dead, including musician Aki Sirkesalo and his family.

FRANCE

Confirmed 95 dead and 189 injured.

GERMANY

Total of 301 confirmed dead and 276 missing.

GREECE

One injured.

HONG KONG

Mixed reports over dead but confirmed at least 21. Number of missing varied from 19 to 72 and as high as 400, with the majority of them, holidaymakers in Thailand.

HUNGARY

Eight injured in Phuket, Thailand.

IRELAND

Two confirmed dead and five missing.

ISRAEL

Six confirmed dead, one missing presumed dead.

ITALY

Reports of 54 dead.

JAPAN

Confirmed 34 dead and ten missing.

LUXEMBOURG

Two dead, a mother and daughter.

MACAU

Six dead in Thailand.

MALAYSIA
Six dead in Thailand.

NETHERLANDS
Confirmed 29 dead and five missing.

NEW ZEALAND
Confirmed three deaths, two women and a man in Thailand. Four others missing presumed dead in Thailand. Around eight injured.

NORWAY
Confirmed 76 dead and eight missing.

PHILIPPINES
Reports of eight dead and some injured in Thailand.

POLAND
Four dead and seven missing. Handful of injured.

PORTUGAL
Four reported dead and four missing.

RUSSIA
Around ten reported dead at Phuket and at least 36 missing.

SINGAPORE
Reports of nine dead across Sri Lanka, India, Indonesia and Thailand.

SOUTH AFRICA
Confirmed 12 dead and three missing presumed dead. Two others died when the wave hit the coast of South Africa.

SOUTH KOREA
Reports of 17 dead and three missing.

SPAIN
One death confirmed and one missing, both in Thailand.

SWEDEN
Suffered one of the greatest foreign fatalities with 544 confirmed dead and 170 missing.

SWITZERLAND
Confirmed 39 dead and 87 missing.

TURKEY
One death in Thailand.

UNITED KINGDOM
Originally said to have suffered 453 fatalities and 95 missing, but this figure was later reduced to 150 missing (by June) 117 confirmed dead. Amongst those who died were Lucy Holland, the 14-year-old granddaughter of film director Richard Attenborough. Her sister Alice, 17, suffered minor injuries. Two other family members reported missing. Fashion photographer Simon Atlee was another fatality. He was on holiday with his Czech girlfriend, model Petra Nemcova (see above) ,who survived the disaster.

UNITED STATES OF AMERICA
Bombarded by some 30,000 inquiries from worried relatives and friends, the State Department vowed: "We will not stop until we know everything we can know."

Initial reports that as many as 2,000 Americans might be dead were mercifully revealed as unfounded. But with so many young backpackers, as well as conventional tourists, traveling through Southeast Asia, the task of allaying the fears of loved ones was monumental.

In early February, the State Department reported that 18 United States citizens had died in the Tsunami and that 15 others were presumed dead. Of the 18 dead, ten were in Thailand and eight in Sri Lanka. Of the 15 presumed dead, 14 were in Thailand and one was in Sri Lanka.

But was that death toll too optimistic? The department's spokesman explained that before listing an American as presumed dead, there had to be "compelling evidence", such as witnesses reporting a person had suddenly disappeared when the disaster struck.

Less encouraging estimates were nevertheless emerging from other sources, and, three months after the Tsunami, it was still being widely reported that there were 135 Americans missing presumed dead, with 34 confirmed dead.

Finally, in mid-July 2005 the State Department stated that the total number of US citizens confirmed as having died in the Tsunami more than six months earlier was 30, with three further Americans still listed as missing presumed dead.

Next page: *Young girls smile and salute for a photo taken January 19, 2005, at one of the camps located in the town of Alue Bilie, Aceh, for civilians displaced by the December 26 Tsunami. Teams from the United Nations (UN) and the World Health Organization (WHO), based aboard USS Abraham Lincoln, were at the time conducting surveys in the region of Aceh, Sumatra, Indonesia to determine the needs of the victims of the Tsunami. U.S. Navy Photo by Photographer's Mate 2nd Class Elizabeth A. Edwards.*